SELF-ESTEEM

Cecil G. Osborne

SELF ESTEEM

Overcoming Inferiority Feelings

ABINGDON PRESS • Nashville

SELF-ESTEEM
Overcoming Inferiority Feelings

Copyright © 1986 by Abingdon Press

Library of Congress Cataloging in Publication Data

OSBORNE, CECIL G.,
　Self-esteem: overcoming inferiority feelings.
　1. Self-respect—Religious aspects—Christianity.
　I. Title.
BV4647.S43Q83　　　　1986　　　　185'1　　　　85-20067

ISBN 0-687-37136-8 *(pbk: alk. paper)*

This book is printed on acid-free paper.

Scripture quotations noted NEB are from The New English
Bible. © the Delegates of the Oxford University Press and the
Syndics of the Cambridge University Press 1961, 1970.
Reprinted by permission.
Those noted NIV are from the Holy Bible: New International
Version Copyright © 1978 by the New York International Bible
Society. Used by permission of Zondervan Bible Publishers.
Those noted KJV are from the King James Version of the Bible.
All others are from the Revised Standard Version of the Bible,
copyrighted 1946, 1952 © 1971, 1973 by the Division of
Christian Education of the National Council of the Churches of
Christ in the U.S.A. and are used by permission.

MANUFACTURED BY THE PARTHENON PRESS AT
NASHVILLE, TENNESSEE, UNITED STATES OF AMERICA

To
My dedicated co-workers at the Burlingame Counseling Center who are providing healing for human hurts in an atmosphere of Christian love—and to the directors of the twenty-eight affiliated centers whose training in Primal Integration and Yokefellow Leadership has enabled them to participate in a remarkable new ministry of healing.

CONTENTS

Introduction...9
Self-Esteem Inventory...13
1. The Sources of Weak Self-Esteem........................15
2. Handling Inferiority and Anger............................31
3. How Feelings of Inferiority
      Reveal Themselves...45
4. Power, Pride, and Inferiority...............................61
5. Guilt and Self-Esteem..73
6. Sex and Self-Esteem..93
7. Self-Esteem and Our Parents.............................107
8. Self-Esteem and Depression...............................125
9. Developing Self-Esteem......................................141
10. The Ultimate Cure...157
Notes..173

A woman was sharing with a small fellowship group a short while after her conversion. "I used to be a terrible neurotic," she said. "Then I was converted, and now . . . I'm a *Christian* neurotic!"

She laughed, and the others joined in. They understood all too well that becoming a Christian does not automatically cure one's neurosis.

In my forty years of pastoral ministry, I experienced a continuing frustration. Although I saw innumerable lives changed in various ways, there were people who continued to suffer from depression, excessive anxiety, and sundry neuroses.

Since my books have been published, several hundred readers have written to tell me of their anguish. Their letters range from single page epistles beginning "Help!" to sixteen pages, describing anxiety, depression, phobias, compulsiveness, impaired relationships, and, in many cases, inferiority, insecurity, and a sense of generalized hopelessness. Most of the letters are from Christians, all of whom reveal a lack of self-esteem.

One typical letter was from a woman who asked, "Where is the abundant life promised us in the Scriptures? After thirty years as a faithful church member, I have never experienced it in the slightest degree." She went on to describe an impoverished, loveless childhood, a deep sense of inferiority, and two divorces. She concluded, "I know I am supposed to believe it, but does God really care?"

A man who had grown up in a home with a punitive father and an unloving mother said that he felt toward God precisely what he had felt toward his father: anger and fear. His judgmental church background did nothing to relieve him of his problem. He had married a woman much like his mother in many ways, and the church to which he belonged was similar to the legalistic one in which he had grown up. Consequently he suffered from a weak sense of identity and deep frustration.

Let us be candid. The regular worship services of a church were never intended to resolve deep-seated emotional problems. Simplistic answers won't suffice. "Pray, read your Bible, meditate, find a place of service," may be well-intentioned pieces of advice for persons with no serious emotional problems, but they are woefully inadequate for people who are still suffering from the effects of a damaging childhood or a traumatic experience in adult life.

A young woman told of having been raped. She felt shattered emotionally when she went to her minister for counseling. He insinuated that she possibly might have invited the attack. Another pastor read her the Scripture passage, "In everything God is at work with those who love him" (Romans 8:28), and assured her that ultimately she would see some good coming from her tragic experience. She was utterly devastated.

Although many people derive benefit from traditional forms of counseling, unfortunately, talk therapy does not always suffice. Insight may on occasion lead to a cure, but it seldom does if the emotional problem has roots that go back to childhood.

This is why, out of a deep sense of frustration with traditional methods, I experimented and explored until I discovered Primal Integration. This is a process whereby we lead people back into their childhood to relive forgotten traumas of the past with as much intensity as they experienced the original event. For hundreds of people, this therapy has been the means of release from hurts buried too deeply for traditional forms of therapy. It provides a new foundation on which a proper self-esteem can be built.

This book deals with ways people are damaged by their early environment and suggests ways of building a healthy self-esteem. All the names used in the incidents described have been changed.

Before you read on, I suggest that you take the following inventory. Though brief, it can help you discover the degree and specific areas of your need. Your score can indicate the amount of effort you will want to expend in developing a greater sense of self-worth.

Cecil G. Osborne, Ph.D., D.D.
Burlingame Counseling Center
19 Park Road
Burlingame CA 94010

Self-Esteem Inventory

On a scale from one to ten, score yourself on the following: (No one else will see your score, so don't make an effort to look better or worse than you are.)

1. My general physical health...................................... ☐
2. My relationship(s) with a person(s)
   of the opposite sex... ☐
3. My relationship with my father as a child.............. ☐
4. The degree of satisfaction
   with my career/daily work................................... ☐
5. My relationship with adult peers........................... ☐
6. My relationship with my mother as a child............ ☐
7. My sense of self-forgiveness................................. ☐
8. My freedom from excessive anxiety...................... ☐
9. My overall financial situation................................ ☐
10. My feeling of being forgiven by God.................... ☐
11. My ability to give love.. ☐
12. My ability to accept compliments easily,
    without embarrassment...................................... ☐
13. My freedom from inferiority feelings................... ☐
14. My ability to forgive readily................................ ☐
15. My freedom from guilt feelings regarding sex....... ☐
16. My love and reverence for God........................... ☐
17. My freedom from guilt over my anger.................. ☐
18. Freedom from depression.................................... ☐
19. The degree to which I usually exhibit
    the Christian virtues.. ☐
20. My self-discipline... ☐

Total .... ——————
Divide by 2 .... ——————
My self-esteem score.... ——————

13

CHAPTER ONE

The Sources of Weak Self-Esteem

The deepest principle in human nature is the craving to be appreciated.

William James

Let me tell you the story of Jane. She was not a particularly appealing young woman, especially since she went to great pains to make herself look unattractive. She used no makeup of any sort and never wore a dress, even to church. She always managed to look scruffy.

Jane was so filled with self-hate, feelings of inferiority, and repressed hostility that it was difficult at first to work with her in counseling sessions. She desperately needed love and attention, but because of her poor self-image, she couldn't accept it even when it was offered.

She lived quite some distance from the Burlingame Counseling Center, and because of irregular bus schedules, it took an entire day for her to get to and from the center where she had her weekly two-hour primal sessions.

Jane had grown up in a home where there was little or no love shown. Her mother was emotionally immature and very self-centered. Her stepfather had molested her sexually when she was a child. Upon graduation from high school, Jane took specialized training and secured a fairly good job, then went to live with a couple who provided a somewhat better environment. The wife was a poor mother substitute, but the husband was understanding and provided Jane with some emotional support.

Between sessions at the center, Jane would phone any of the therapists she could reach several times a week, often in a panic. She needed frequent reassurance that we cared. In a sharing group which she attended along with her primal sessions, she would occasionally leave the group in hysterics, lock herself in the restroom, and threaten suicide. On one occasion, she broke a light bulb and made a rather serious attempt to slash her wrists with the broken glass. Jane was obviously in bad shape.

However, she proved to be an excellent subject for Primal Integration. Each week, for two hours, she relived the repressed memories of her unhappy childhood. There were tears of hurt and anger, but it was several months before the full force of the rage against her parents emerged. One usually experiences primal hurt and fear first, and only when these feelings are discharged begins to feel whatever anger may be lying beneath the hurt.

For six months there seemed little improvement, but Jane had one powerful trait working for her; she had perseverance. She was a very determined young woman. We began to see progress during the ninth month. From then on, her growth was remarkable. At the end of the year she terminated her therapy sessions and decided to move into her own apartment. With glowing self-confidence she bought furniture, decorated her new home, and proceeded to begin life anew.

A CHANGED PERSONALITY

It was a totally new Jane who returned three months later to report on her progress. She radiated confidence and self-assurance. The once sloppily dressed Jane now wore a very becoming outfit. Among other things, she reported that she was beginning to wear dresses on occasion, evidence of a growing acceptance of her femininity. She told us about a recent promotion and her tentative plans for seeking an entirely new career. It was a radical transformation mentally, spiritually, and physically. Her complexion was better, her posture had improved, and she exuded great self-confidence.

But one of the most amazing evidences of her growth had to do with her relationship with her mother. During the year of her therapy when she had seen her mother, she would cross to the other side of the street and avert her gaze. Now she sought out her mother and had a face-to-face confrontation with her. She told her how much she had hated her, but the hostility was all gone. She expressed a desire to establish a new mother-daughter relationship. On the verge of tears, Jane's mother told her how badly she felt about not having been an adequate parent. At this point, Jane began to minister to her mother and, in effect, became her mother's counselor.

Next, without any suggestion or guidance from us, she sought out her brother and sisters, with whom she had had impaired relationships. Jane made a diligent effort to get on a new footing with each member of the family.

When she first came to us, Jane had been attending a legalistic, fundamentalist church, where she frequently felt judged. We encouraged her to search for a different type of church. She did so and located a Christian fellowship of loving people. They genuinely cared about her. She had grown up in a rejecting, judgmental home, and the last thing she needed was a church family that was rigid and unloving.

Less than a year and a half after ending her therapy, Jane showed up at the center with a fine looking young man she had met at church. They are now married.

HOW JANE DID IT

How did Jane do it? What are the factors involved in the complete transformation of a young woman who had experienced a lifetime of rejection?

First, she had the determination to seek intensive therapy and was not expecting a sudden miraculous cure for a lifetime of hurt.

Second, at the counseling center, she found total, unconditional acceptance, regardless of her insatiable demands and neurotic behavior.

Third, she had the courage to relive the tragedy of her childhood, trauma by trauma, week after week, for something like fifty sessions. By discharging the hurts and fears and repressed anger, she became able to give and receive love for the first time in her life.

Fourth, the warm, accepting atmosphere in her new church provided the emotional climate in which her growth could be enhanced.

Jane reported to me that the time and money she spent on Primal Integration therapy was the best investment she could ever hope to make, because it changed her from a self-hating young woman with a crippling inferiority complex into a self-accepting, loving, successful person.

She is just one of several hundred people who have come from twenty-nine states and twelve foreign countries for Primal Integration therapy. From places as distant as Australia, New Zealand, and Hong Kong, they have come in increasing numbers in order to relive, and thus discharge, the buried hurts of childhood.

A quiet, diffident young man who came for Primal Integration told us how he happened to be there. He said,

> I was vacationing in Hawaii. Each morning when I went into the coffee shop for breakfast, I sat close to a rack of books

and magazines. My eye kept falling on a paperback titled, *The Art of Learning to Love Yourself* by Cecil Osborne. I wanted to buy that book, but I was too embarrassed to pick it up. Because of my extreme self-consciousness, I was afraid of what people would think if I picked it up and took it to the cashier. Finally, my desire to read it and learn how to love myself, which I certainly didn't at that point, overcame my timidity. I bought it. And that's where I first learned about your therapy.

He was so intrigued with the process that he asked if he could take the training and become a Primal Integration therapist. His background and experience qualified him, and now that he had new self-esteem, he succeeded in becoming a successful primal facilitator.

SELF-ALIENATION BEGINS IN CHILDHOOD

What is the source of the deep sense of inferiority and lack of confidence that young man experienced in Hawaii? What is it that makes some people happy extroverts and renders others timid, withdrawn, and inadequate?

We can only speculate as to the part heredity plays in the process, since it would vary from person to person; we do know without a doubt what environmental factors create neurosis.

We have listened for thousands of hours as men and women, from age sixteen to seventy-five, have relived the forgotten traumas of childhood that robbed them of their self-esteem.

Remember that about 99 percent of all that transpired in your life before the age of five has been forgotten by the conscious mind; yet it was during those crucial years that your personality was formed. This is not speculation or theory; we have heard the wails and sobs of people reliving those forgotten years and have observed the sense of relief they experience as a result.

Of course, it is not only what happened to a child that produces the hurt; it is how that child *perceived* the situation or incident. To illustrate:

It was at the end of the school year. The parents were gathered in the school auditorium to hear their small progeny demonstrate newly acquired skills. Jimmy had excelled in music and was to play a piano number he had practiced diligently. But when he marched out onto the stage, he was seized with panic, and after two or three fumbling chords, he fled in haste. On the way home, his devastated parents kept repeating, "Oh, Jimmy, you let us down; you let us down!"

Jim was in his early thirties when he relived that event with every bit as much shame and horror as when it had originally happened. His parents, of course, had almost forgotten the event, but it was embedded into that eight-year-old emotional structure.

Jimmy could never be induced to touch the piano again. More important, he remained convinced that there was never anything he could do to make it up to his parents. For over twenty years, he had lived with a largely buried sense of shame and embarrassment, and a consequent sense of inadequacy, originating at age eight. He experienced in his primal sessions the buried emotion, "I failed them; they don't love me; they will never love me again. I can never expect love from anyone because I am so unworthy. I'm a failure."

Yes, Jimmy was a very sensitive boy. He blew that one incident out of all proportion, one might say. But that was the kind of a boy he was. His parents loved him devotedly and never would have intentionally harmed him. They meant well, but the damage was done. He lived with a deep sense of inferiority and insecurity, until he was able to discharge the hurt and shame in a series of primal sessions. There were other hurts, too, of course, but that one stood out.

In most instances, it is not one big trauma, but innumerable lesser ones that cause the damage.

A man from Europe wrote,

> At forty-two, I am desperate about my state of mind and health. I am the only son of a highly possessive mother and rejecting father. Cuddling and holding me? I can't remember that from either parent. The only way I could sometimes get their acclaim was through academic achievement. No wonder I got stuck into liquor at age twenty, married against their wishes at twenty-one (by which time I was already a full-blown alcoholic), divorced at twenty-six, remarried at twenty-six, turned to Alcoholics Anonymous at twenty-eight.
>
> I wrote and attained my Ph.D. [in literature] during a relatively sober period of three months when I was courting my second wife, became full professor and chairman of my department.
>
> But in spite of my being sober for more than fourteen years, in spite of my academic success, my beautiful and loving wife and my three nice children, a beautiful home in God-given surroundings, I feel depressed most of the time—seething with anger from I don't know where, often feeling completely worthless. I suffer from an acid stomach, a spastic colon, bad digestion, continuous headaches and profuse perspiration. When my wife tells me that she loves me, I have often asked her why, because I can't get along with myself most of the time.

He asked how soon he could be accepted for Primal Integration therapy. That is a graphic illustration of one of the ways a person can become neurotic and develop a poor self-image.

HOW A CHILD DERIVES SELF-WORTH

Children who are criticized often and receive little praise or affirmation come to feel inadequate, unworthy, and generally inferior. They have no way to derive a sense of self-worth except from the most important people in their lives—their parents. If they do not receive enough love and affirmation together with holding and cuddling, they grow up with a weak sense of self-esteem. Dr. Haim Ginott writes:

> When a child is in the midst of strong emotions, he cannot listen to anyone. He cannot accept advice or consolation or constructive criticism. He wants us to understand him. He wants us to understand what is going on inside himself at that particular moment. Furthermore, he wants to be understood without having to disclose fully what he is experiencing. It is a game in which he reveals only a little of what he feels, needing to have us guess the rest.
>
> When a child tells us "The teacher spanked me," we do not have to ask him for more details, nor do we need to say, "What did you do to deserve it? If a teacher spanked you, you must have done something. What did you do?" We don't even have to say, "Oh, I'm so sorry." We need to show him that we understand his pain and embarrassment and feelings of revenge. How do we know what he feels? We look at him and listen to him, and also draw on our own emotional experience. We know what a child *must* feel when he is shamed in public in the presence of peers. We so phrase our words that the child knows we understand what he has gone through. Any of the following statements would serve well:
>
> 1. It must have been embarrassing.
> 2. It must have made you furious.
> 3. You must have hated the teacher at that moment.
> 4. It must have hurt your feelings terribly.
> 5. It was a bad day for you, wasn't it?

A child's strong feelings do not disappear when he is told "It's not nice to feel that way," or when the parents try to convince him that he has no reason to feel that way. Strong feelings do not vanish by being banished; they do diminish in intensity and lose their sharp edges when the listener accepts them with sympathy and understanding.[1]

Unfortunately, a vast majority of children are told that they "shouldn't" feel that way. Their feelings are not validated, and as a consequence, they repress their basic emotions.

In a therapy session, a young man relived an experience when he was about four or five years old. He had been playing outdoors and wanted to go inside. The door was locked, so he rang the bell, then pounded vociferously on the door. He said, "I don't know how long I stood there, hammering on the door. It seemed forever. Eventually, my father opened the door, looked out, and asked, 'Oh, did you want to come in?' I was angry, and said, 'Yes, you fool!' "

"My mother said reproachfully, 'Son, Jesus said that anyone calling a person a fool was in danger of hellfire. Don't ever do that again.' Well, for years I lived in mortal fear of being plunged into a fiery hell because I'd called my dad a fool."

It must be reemphasized—it is the child's perception that matters. The mother's intention was simply to correct the little boy's manner of expressing himself, and she used the Bible to emphasize the point. Unfortunately, the threat fell on fertile ground.

When a child is emotionally upset, *any* threat or criticism is absorbed much more quickly into the emotional structure. In many instances it leaves a permanent scar.

HOW INFERIORITY AND INSECURITY BEGIN

Feelings of insecurity and inferiority are transmitted not only verbally, but nonverbally. They can be caught by osmosis. Children absorb every nuance from their immediate environment. They are fantastic observers, but, unfortunately, poor interpreters.

In addition to childhood inputs, there is now a vast body of evidence that the unborn child experiences the mother's emotions. One young woman had a crippling anxiety neurosis that prevented her from holding a job or functioning normally in society. Though there had been an absence of warm affection from her father, there seemed to be no early experience sufficiently devastating to account for her enormous anxiety. In a long-distance telephone conversation with her mother I asked, "What were you experiencing during your pregnancy with Nancy?" She thought for a moment then said, "Oh! I was very upset most of the time when I was carrying her. My husband was away from home a great deal; we moved several times during that period, and I was filled with deep anxiety."

In addition to the generalized anxiety the mother felt during her pregnancy, there had been one terrifying incident in which she had seen a prowler just outside her bedroom window. She was alone at the time. Here, then, were the roots of the daughter's crippling anxiety. She was being bathed in it during the entire nine months in utero. The unborn infant is part and parcel of a mother's body and emotions. Negative emotions such as sustained fear, anxiety, and anger produce a negative emotional effect in an unborn child.

Anthropologist Ashley Montagu of Harvard states that the evidence supports the hypothesis that stressful emotions in pregnant women are quite capable of affecting the unborn child in various ways. He added that maternal attitudes of acceptance, rejection, or indifference to their pregnancy can well mean the difference in some cases between adequate and inadequate development of the fetus.

Angie, a college dropout, came from another state for three weeks or more of intensive primal sessions. Unfortunately, she was a very poor subject. She was not only severely neurotic; her attention span was incredibly short. We found it extremely difficult to work with her, partly because she was unable to cooperate, but chiefly because of her incredible anxiety. She could not remain in one position for more than ten seconds.

Her mother revealed that during the entire time she was carrying Angie, she had undergone a vast deal of stress. When she described it in detail, we could begin to understand why her daughter drank to excess and was so severely neurotic.

Angie said on numerous occasions, "I never know for sure whether I want to be a saint or a slut—maybe a teacher or maybe a writer." Though she was prepsychotic, and in spite of the extreme difficulty of working with her, she made significant progress and is now back in college, functioning much better.

There was another important aspect to her emotional illness. Angie had never known any limits. Her parents were overly permissive. And, of course, a child with no limits feels unloved and thus is filled with anxiety.

Brad was a quiet, amiable, rather passive young man outwardly. However, he went on periodic drunks and invariably ended by getting into barroom brawls. On one occasion, it took four policemen to get him into a patrol car.

Brad's father had had a severe drug problem, and of course, had little or no time for him. Worse, his stepmother beat him regularly with sadistic delight. He had never received the slightest morsel of love from either parent.

After his first series of Primal Integration sessions, Brad wrote:

I'm beginning now to see everything in a new and different way. I'm not fleeing from my loneliness to obsessive socializing. I feel now that I can choose to socialize or not. I'm beginning to feel that what I say and feel are much more in harmony than they were. And, more important, I feel more positive about my future. There is less tension and apprehension. Among other things, I find that my appetite is better, and I am beginning to slow down. For several years I've eaten only one meal a day. Now I'm hungry all the time.

I now feel that I want to develop a meaningful relationship with women, instead of just using them as I've always done. The goddess-bitch complex is being resolved. I am starting to see women as women, not as the unattainable goddess, the loving mother I didn't have, or as the bitch mother, my stepmother. I'm beginning for the first time to see women as persons, not just physical beings.

Another thing: I plan to shave off my beard soon. I don't need it. I'd like to look as good outwardly as I feel inside. There's no longer that compulsive need to look scruffy all the time. You know, I feel sorry for my parents. There's almost no anger toward them now. I feel I could hug my father now and tell him, "It's okay, Dad," only I know he wouldn't understand. He's had four marriages, and with his alcohol and drug background, he's terribly neurotic. He probably won't ever change.

And something else: I am beginning to feel strongly that I am driving, instead of being driven. In other words, I am feeling less compulsive. Today during a long walk I stopped in at a nearby church. I sat in the sanctuary for a bit and looked at the cross up in front. I began to see the meaning of the cross. I can't hate anymore. All my anger isn't gone. Perhaps I'm not supposed to be totally without anger, but it isn't going to drive me as it has in the past.

Brad had two more weeks of daily therapy. During the final two sessions, the last of his hurt and fear came up.

There was a burst of violent anger. He erupted in rage toward his sadistic stepmother. It lasted a long time.

Finally, exhausted, he fell back and said, "It's all over. I'm cleaned out. Everything, *everything's* going to be different now."

We didn't hear from Brad for several months. Then, without warning, he dropped in one day with a lovely young woman.

"I just wanted you to meet her," he said. "I am now capable, for the first time in my life, of a sustained, gratifying relationship with a woman. *This* relationship's going to last." There was a look of peace and quiet assurance as he said it. Somehow, he was utterly believable and delightful.

Unavoidable Damage to the Child

Shana was sixteen when I first saw her briefly at a social function at her parents' home in another state. She was beautiful, troublesome, and rebellious. I did not see her again until her parents called me to say that Shana, now twenty-seven, was living nearby and needed counseling.

In the years since I had seen her, she had left home, held numerous jobs—some of them very good ones—changed residences with great frequency, and, most unfortunate of all, was attracting one loser after another.

In our first counseling session, I learned that she had been born with a physical malfunction which necessitated a body cast shortly after birth. She was in that cast for what seemed ages to her. In her early primals, she began to relive being in that restrictive body cast. She was in rebellion against the restraint. Little or no movement was possible. At a time when an infant needs to stretch and move arms and legs, she was immobilized. Thus began her rebellion against all restriction. She began to see that her rebellious nature had a legitimate origin. Too, there had been a difficult birth. She relived all this and discharged the repressed anger encapsulating those infant frustrations. After her Primal Integration sessions, she joined a Yokefellow sharing group conducted at the center. She felt a need for the support of a caring group of people, as well as the insight and spiritual growth engendered by such a group.

Masochism, a manifestation of self-hate, is a very difficult emotion to eradicate. It often begins in some form of anguish, frustration, or failure. Shana had definitely been masochistic. It took the form of becoming failure-prone and being attracted to losers. This was a trait she could see in herself, but without being able to change it.

No form of therapy we are currently aware of has the slightest chance of helping a masochist except Primal Integration. Even so, it can be a fairly lengthy process. It is as if the masochistic person were literally programmed for failure, having been aimed inexorably in that direction by some malevolent combination of forces. Shana has experienced remarkable healing and growth as a result of her primal sessions and a Yokefellow group. She now functions beautifully.

A SELF-FULFILLING PROPHECY

Children who are constantly criticized come to believe that they are unlovable. If they do not receive love in a form they can accept, they feel, "I must be worthless, or they would love me, care for me, hold me." Holding is a physical manifestation of caring. Children who receive little or no touching inevitably feel rejected and thus unworthy: "If I am worthless, then I am not worthy of success." The battered children—and there are millions of them—usually grow up with monumental feelings of unworthiness and vague, diffused senses of shame or guilt.

Though it is seldom dealt with, the following emotions all have a common denominator:

Failure	Shame	Rejection	Inadequacy
Guilt	Unworthiness	Inferiority	

One who as a child *felt* loved and affirmed seldom experiences any of those seven manifestations of weak self-esteem; for as psychiatrist Karl Menninger has said, "Love is the medicine for the healing of the world."

CHAPTER TWO

Handling Inferiority and Anger

I shall tell you a great secret, my friend. Do not wait for the last judgment; it takes place every day.

Albert Camus

PASSIVITY AND INFERIORITY

There are several possible avenues open to people who, as children, felt rejected and unloved. If passive, they may become quiet and withdrawn, or even antisocial. Their repressed anger produces a kind of all-pervasive anxiety or depression, sometimes a combination of both.

The passive-*dependent* male tends to marry a woman who is very strong, who will presumably protect him, and thus become the "good mother" to his inner child, as opposed to the "bad mother" from whom he felt only rejection. (The same applies for the passive-dependent female.)

The passive-*aggressive* male will tend to marry a combination of the competent and nurturing mother-wife. Not realizing that his enormous need for nurturing is rooted in childhood feelings of rejection by his mother, he will now make incessant demands on his wife for more love, more sympathy, and more attention. His unrealistic expectations may drive his wife into depression, despair, or divorce. His unmet childhood need for love is added to his legitimate adult expectations. When his neurotic needs are not met, he will often become irrationally angry. Ted is a good example. After his primal experience, he wrote:

> I discovered in my sessions that many of my emotions were either repressed or distorted because of experiences in my childhood and adolescent years. My basic feeling has been one of inferiority and inadequacy, lack of self-confidence, insecurity, and a lack of self-assurance.
>
> By reliving childhood experiences, I got in touch with these emotions. I relived the feeling of being neglected by my demanding mother. I felt I could never please her and was assured that I would cause her to go to an early grave. She was always critical of my friends and their parents. As a result, I felt that I was doing something wrong to cause this kind of response. She seldom gave me any affection, and on occasion whipped my brother and me mercilessly. I developed the feeling that I was no good, worthless.
>
> I relived in primal sessions the buried feeling that my father favored my older brother, who resembled him physically. I looked more like my mother, but didn't particularly want to be like her. The favoritism shown my brother caused me to feel I wasn't good enough to merit my father's love and attention.
>
> When I was eight years old, I was beaten up by an older boy. I went to my father for consolation. His response was, "Don't expect me to fight your battles." I was stunned, lost, hurt, and felt very much alone and rejected. From then on, I was very reluctant ever to ask my father for anything. I felt I was a mistake and should never have been named Ted, Jr.
>
> I saw clearly in my primal sessions how I was emotionally damaged by such experiences, and how, as a result of feeling unloved, I had shut down on my feelings.
>
> I can see how my anger stemmed from my feelings of rejection, inadequacy, and inferiority. I felt a misfit. I desperately wanted to prove my worth, but didn't know how,

or was afraid to find out. I withdrew into myself, and said, "Someday, I'll show you all."

My anger toward my wife stemmed from those feelings. I relived some of my encounters with her and saw how I had made her the recipient of my hostile feelings of inferiority and self-hate.

Now I feel that I am an adequate human being, that I have good qualities, that I am worthy and have a great deal to offer. I no longer need to depend on others for my "good feelings." Since my primal experience, I have grown beyond the place where I need to have my parents love me. It would have been nice if they had been able to do so, but I realize now that it wasn't my fault, as I had thought as a child. I don't need them to validate me now.

Being alone now does not make me feel rejected or depressed. This has been the greatest experience of my life, because in a relatively short time, I have been able to resolve some things that have bothered me and adversely affected me all my life. Revisiting those childhood scenes and reliving the traumas of childhood has been painful but soothing. I can now see the true colors of nature better, among other things.

I feel relieved, joyous, emotionally strengthened and self-assured. I am able to think intelligently. I feel open and can express my feelings. I am now able to listen with understanding. In those primal sessions, I gained the equivalent of many years of wisdom and insight.

That is the experience of a passive-aggressive man—passive in that he accepted his childhood hurts without rebelling and acquired feelings of inferiority and helplessness—aggressive in that he projected his primal feelings of repressed anger onto his wife.

AGGRESSIVENESS AND INFERIORITY

Aggressive people who develop feelings of inferiority in childhood may react in one of several ways:

If they have a good intellect and creativity, they will find a way to compensate for their sense of inadequacy. Alfred Adler, an early disciple of Freud's, felt overshadowed by his older brother, George, who was outgoing, highly intelligent, and popular. Alfred, on the contrary, felt quite inadequate in social situations and, consequently, resolved to find some way he could compensate. He had a good mind and decided to excel in school. He became a brilliant student.

In later years his brother George was heard to say, when his famous brother's name came into the discussion, "I never could see what people saw in Alfred."

People with a severe inferiority complex, unless they have learned how to compensate satisfactorily, can become quite defensive. Such people, for instance, find it almost impossible to say "I was wrong." Self-accepting persons can utter those three magic words without difficulty when they see that, like all humans, they have been mistaken. Defensive, insecure people often refuse to seek professional help for emotional problems or to resolve marital difficulties. They cannot admit they might be wrong.

An aggressive young man who came to this country with twenty dollars and managed to amass a fortune revealed his sense of insecurity by an insatiable need to talk about himself. I came to understand the reason when he told me one day that he was thirty years old before his father, visiting here for the first time, gave him a very mild compliment. He said, "That was the first kind word my father ever said to me."

His compulsive need to talk was a manifestation of need for attention. His wife, a lovely woman with her own deep feelings of inferiority, showed her sense of inadequacy by her steadfast refusal ever to admit having made a mistake. Such people manage to mask their lack of self-worth in this way. They dare not admit even to themselves the extent of their self-rejection.

Creative people manage to compensate for their childhood hurts or limitations in various ways.

Naturalist Charles Darwin did so poorly in school that his father once told him, "You will be a disgrace to yourself and all your family." Gilbert (G.K.) Chesterton, the English writer, didn't learn to read until he was eight years old. One of his teachers told him, "If we could open your head, we should not find any brain, but only a lump of fat." Thomas Edison's first teacher described him as "addled," and his father almost convinced him that he was a dunce.

Albert Einstein's parents feared their child was very dull. He performed so badly in high school, except in mathematics, that a teacher asked him to drop out, telling him, "You will never amount to anything, Albert." Einstein once said, "My parents were worried because I started talking comparatively late, and they consulted a doctor because of it." None of his teachers ever recognized his potential. One of them said, "Your very presence spoils the respect of the class for me." Albert accepted the suggestion that he leave the class, and he spent many months wandering through northern Italy, a high school dropout of the 1890s. He supported himself with odd jobs and was several times passed over for positions for which he applied. It was while he was working as an examiner of patents at the Swiss patent office that he began to do the initial thinking that led him to develop the theory of relativity.

These people and a host of others discovered how to take the rebuffs of childhood and compensate for the feelings of rejection and self-hate. There is now considerable evidence, as Adler suggested, that a moderate amount of inferiority can be a powerful stimulus to achievement. Too great a feeling of inadequacy, however, can be crushing.

All people are, or feel themselves to be, inadequate in some way, but I have known numerous people whose deep sense of inferiority was never fully resolved, despite great achievements.

THE LASTING EFFECTS OF INFERIORITY

I recall a man of considerable wealth who had once been strikingly handsome. He was an outstanding public speaker and a dynamic personality. Yet when he had too much to drink, he was known to fall on the floor in the presence of guests and loudly boast of his wealth and his great achievements. Only when alcohol released his inhibitions did he reveal his deep sense of inferiority. He had grown up in abject poverty and felt inferior to his fellow students who came from better homes. His significant attainments as an adult had not succeeded in erasing from his consciousness the sense of shame over his childhood deprivation. He had absorbed from his father, a day laborer, enormous feelings of inferiority.

One may compensate for a deep sense of insecurity, but in some degree the feelings are still there, concealed beneath the facade. I knew a well-educated woman who had as her guest a friend from out of town. The friend, whom I knew, had invited my wife and me to dinner at a local restaurant. Her hostess, in the pangs of a possessive jealousy, did not speak to her for three days and ultimately severed the relationship. In such ways do ancient insecurities manifest themselves.

When you recognize that the vast majority of people have some degree of inferiority, insecurity, inadequacy, or self-rejection, you will be able to cope more successfully with your own.

INFERIORITY AND SADOMASOCHISM

I have discussed the types of women a man tends to marry when he has strong feelings of inferiority. Let's take a look at the kind of husband a typical woman may choose if she feels inferior or insecure.

Depending upon circumstances and various childhood factors, she unconsciously may seek a man who appears strong and competent. Most women want chiefly two things in a man: strength with gentleness. The terribly insecure woman needs this strength, only more so. She may find such a man whose strength is tempered with tenderness and consideration, or she may marry one whose facade seems to promise strength, but who is inwardly very weak.

Sometimes a woman marries a passive man who is quiet and undemonstrative, because she fears that a stronger man will trigger the fear of her own father. All this takes place at a totally unconscious level, of course.

A woman who has grown up in a home where little or no love was expressed, and who feels unworthy as a consequence, may become masochistic. Such a woman usually finds a sadist who will beat her down, either physically, verbally, or both.

Mary received no love from her mother as a child, and only curt indifference from her father. She was a sitting duck for the first sadist who came along. Sadism does not spring out of strength, but out of weakness. Her husband was a weak, passive-aggressive alcoholic.

Bill's sadomasochism did not express itself in acts of violence. His was a more subtle and deadly approach. He used sarcasm to cut her down, and when he had been drinking, became very abusive verbally. In a counseling session Mary told in a martyred tone of voice how many nights she had cried herself to sleep. She had extracted promises from him a hundred times that he would stop drinking. But, of course, these were empty commitments. Bill was a loser, with enormous feelings of inferiority and worthlessness. Like most masochistic persons, he simply projected his self-hate onto her.

Through counseling sessions and participation in a Yokefellow sharing group, Mary eventually gained enough self-respect and courage to deliver an ultimatum. "Either you start going to AA and stop drinking and abusing me, or I will get a divorce."

Bill, of course, had no intention of going to AA. He needed alcohol as a tranquilizer, to deaden the pain of his miserable childhood.

Mary eventually divorced him, and in a year or two was happily married to a splendid man who possessed quiet strength and gentleness. These were the qualities she had thought Bill possessed when she married him twenty-five unhappy years earlier.

As Sigmund Freud pointed out, in adult life we try to solve the problems originating in childhood. The reason for the unhappy marriage Mary and Bill endured for a quarter of a century was that both had been damaged in childhood. Each had a hurting little inner child in need of nurture and tenderness. Bill married Mary because he perceived in her a weak woman who would not threaten his insecurities. Mary saw in Bill a gentle, passive person. Being quiet, she felt, he would not be like her gruff, rejecting father. But since at least 85 percent of our decisions, major and minor, are made at an unconscious level, neither Bill nor Mary was consciously aware of what it was they were blindly seeking in each other.

Immaturity and Oversensitivity

Nearly everyone, of course, has islands of immaturity. The Bible declares, "All have sinned and fall short of the glory of God" (Romans 3:23). Well-intentioned parents sin against their children. Thus we could add to the Apostle Paul's declaration the statement that most of us have been sinned against more than we have sinned. We have been damaged by our parents in some degree. They were sinned against by their parents and warped by society's false values.

As all have sinned, we have in turn sinned against one another. We end as damaged souls, each with certain areas of weakness and insecurity, or pride and arrogance.

I think of a man with a magnificent mind and a striking personality. He is an outstanding speaker and religious leader. His mother saw some of this potential in him and through overmothering and fatuous praise engendered in him an overweening pride and intellectual arrogance. Her excessive pride in her brilliant son marred an otherwise delightful personality. Even the best of us are defective in some degree.

Oversensitivity is one manifestation of our inferiority and insecurity. Everyone can be offended by criticism or rejection. It is normal to be capable of having our feelings hurt. To be otherwise would render us insensitive to our own emotions and the needs of others. But one who has a deep sense of insecurity can become hypersensitive. The slightest criticism can devastate such a person. A less sensitive individual may offer such advice as, "You mustn't be so thin-skinned," which is on a par with telling a person with a migraine headache not to hurt so much. We each have a right to our islands of immaturity. We came by them as the result of our childhood inputs.

Does this justify our remaining in our impaired condition or blaming our parents? Not at all! Nor are we to blame ourselves. The goal is to become aware of our defects, to accept them as a reality, and begin to work on those aspects of our personality that need attention.

INSECURITY AND THE NEED FOR POWER

The need for power is a common manifestation of inferiority. It is understandable when we realize that insecure people feel safe when they can control their environment. There is the man who rules his family with an iron hand and a loud voice. As indicated at the beginning of this chapter, the lust for power is rooted not in strength, but in weakness.

Feeling vulnerable if they are not ruling their immediate environment, weak but aggressive people conceal their insecurities from themselves and others by dominating those about them.

They may do this by shouting commands, criticisms, or with the cutting edge of sarcasm. They may develop personality traits that send out a silent threat to anyone who dares challenge them. It is possible to control through silence, just as readily as with angry threats.

Few women use money as power, but most men who have acquired a fortune are seldom content; they usually strive for a still greater fortune. Money represents power, and this can quell one's all-pervasive sense of powerlessness and insecurity.

Even the religiously motivated are not immune from the lust for power. I recall an able, conscientious religious leader who became the administrative head of a large denomination. His health was beginning to fail. He told me that he felt himself slipping, both mentally and physically. I urged him to accept a position in an advisory capacity, with less of an administrative load. I added, "You will probably be dead within three years at the rate you're going."

But power and prestige are alluring goals. He hung on to his position for another two years and died in his fifties of a heart attack.

Pride, prominence, prestige, and power are all related, and of the seven deadly sins, pride heads the list.

In another chapter, I deal with the almost universal, though unconscious desire to "recapture the rapture" of early childhood, when the infant ruled his or her tiny realm. Just for a moment, see if you can sense in yourself the security you get when you are in complete control of your immediate environment. Or, if you have never achieved this, try to imagine what it would be like to be in charge, to be able to direct and dominate others.

Hitler's psychopathic drive to rule the world sprang, not from inner strength but from a sense of powerlessness. He had been a total failure until he discovered he had the ability to arouse the emotions of others. The Germans at that point, having lost World War I, felt vanquished and vulnerable. Hitler seized upon their feelings of powerlessness and whipped up their anger over being alleged victims of hostile world powers. Their sense of helplessness and failure—and their consequent lust for power—were the sparks that set the world on fire.

An aggressive woman, no less than a man, can enjoy the feeling of power that comes from controlling her environment. The wife of a prominent citizen came to see me some years ago, soon after the death of her husband. She was in tears as she talked. It seems that her husband had died of a stroke while mowing the lawn. Wringing her hands in anguish she said, "I think perhaps I killed him. I have enormous energy, but he seemed rather listless to me. I like a very active social life and am always busy at half a dozen things. Weekends, when my husband insisted on relaxing, I had him mowing the lawn, though we could well afford a gardener. I *made* him do the gardening, and it was while mowing the lawn that he died. I think I killed him. He often said that I was happy only when he was frantically doing the gardening, repairing the house, or attending cocktail parties. I've talked to two psychiatrists, a psychologist, four pastors, and many friends, asking them if they think I killed my husband." The tears were coming faster now.

"Do you think I did? Do you? Tell me, I need to know."

"What have the others told you?"

"They all said that I was not responsible for his death, but I'm not so sure. . . . Do you think . . . ?"

Quite obviously she felt responsible for his death. Nothing that any of her friends or counselors had told her had alleviated her sense of culpability. I had neither a desire to add to her guilt nor to pronounce her innocent. I sensed that no matter what I said, she would continue to make the rounds, trying to find some fragile evidence to prove that she was not guilty, as she knew she was. As gently as I could, I said, "Perhaps we can never know for sure, but you must cease punishing yourself."

Hard-driving persons cannot understand why everyone else isn't as energetic as they. More passive individuals strike them as indolent, lacking in drive and ambition. A woman associate of mine once said to me when I had been vigorously attacked by an irate woman, "The only way to fight an angry woman is with your hat. Grab it and run." That is precisely what many men do—realizing there is no sense in fighting a losing battle.

But there are other ways aggressive women seek to control. Some are very subtle and manipulative. I once knew a charming woman who had a host of friends. Her husband was the executive vice-president of an international corporation and a man of tremendous ability. He retired, a vigorous sixty-five-year-old man, in perfect health. His wife manipulated him into a retirement home, in which he had not the slightest interest. It was the last important victory she won in forty years of sweet, firm manipulation. He died two years after retirement, a victim, his friends said, of having no other way to escape the gentle, inexorable dominance of a firm-minded wife.

PRIDE AND ANGER

The lust for power, born in weakness or the fear of being vulnerable, is also a manifestation of pride. Pride will not allow one to admit that he or she is wrong. Prideful persons cannot endure the thought of failure, either in an argument, in sports, or in any aspect of life. They must always be right, must inevitably win, be ever in control. It was for his pride in challenging God's final authority that Lucifer, the most beautiful of all the angels, was cast out of heaven. We now know him as Satan, the eternal adversary of God. He is not only the father of lies, as the Bible states, but the father of pride.

Great men, like lesser mortals, have their points of pride. Sigmund Freud, according to one of his biographers, had his vulnerable points. Criticism of his theories hurt him a great deal, and when Jung and Adler defected and started their own schools of thought, Freud reacted with indignation, hurt, and anger.

One of the least recognized facts in today's society is that most depression stems from repressed anger. Earl was an able, attractive personality who had amassed a fortune and retired at age fifty. Just as he was beginning to relish a life of ease, his wife demanded that he move out of the house.

The wife was seeing a psychologist friend of mine, and Earl was counseling with me. He had an insatiable need to be mothered, never having received sufficient love from his own mother. In business, he was competent and aggressive. In his relationship with women, he was passive and

demanding. His wife understandably announced that she
wanted to be his wife, not his mother. His vast need for
nurturance in every form was so great that his wife ended
the marriage out of frustration.

When I first saw Earl, he was seeing a psychiatrist who
had prescribed medication for his depression, a minister
who gave him some emotional support, an attorney friend
who provided a kindly listening ear, and a business friend
who heard him out. Because of a deprived childhood, Earl
was a love addict, a bottomless pit. He was getting
nurturance from these various people and still pleading for
his wife to take him back.

I explained to him that it was anger at his wife, rooted in
repressed anger at his mother, which had caused his
depression. "No," Earl said, "it is just hurt, not anger."

There was hurt, of course, but his inner child was
reacting in anger to an unloving mother-wife. Instead of
letting himself feel the understandable childhood anger
over being rejected by his mother, he could feel only the
depression, resulting from buried anger.

In counseling sessions, Earl tried to get in touch with
those buried emotions, but because they were so repressed,
he never touched on them. He could not let himself feel the
buried anger. Eventually, he recovered somewhat from his
depression and began to seek love elsewhere. At last report,
he was planning to marry a mature, nurturing woman who
can probably be the wife-*mother* he seeks. The relationship
looks promising, though it required many counseling
sessions to bring about.

CHAPTER THREE

How Feelings of Inferiority Reveal Themselves

Many people stand on a moral staircase, criticizing the person on the step below, and skeptical of the one on the step above.

Gabriel Montalban

It may come as a surprise to those suffering from a full-blown inferiority complex to learn that many of the great achievers of history experienced vast feelings of inadequacy, self-doubt and failure. One of the greatest dancers of all time was Vaslav Nijinsky. Alfred Adler's biography of him was suppressed for many years because Nijinsky's wife rejected a less-than-glorious description of her husband. Adler described how the dancer's great ability was not matched by an equally strong ego structure. He fell from the heights of fame in 1917 to the depths of schizophrenic desolation. The world could never satisfy Nijinsky's vast need for approval and adulation, and to cover his feelings of inferiority, he developed messianic strivings. He died insane—a combination of enormous talent and a deep sense of inferiority.

To know that you are talented, beautiful, gifted, brilliant, or a great achiever is not always enough to compensate for deeply rooted feelings of self-hate for not having achieved enough.

For example, Sigmund Freud's biographers point out that between the ages of thirty-four and forty-four he suffered from depression, was addicted to cocaine, and had a strong dependence on the rather strange Wilhelm Fliess. Freud also suffered from migraine headaches and heart palpitations, which are usually associated with emotional problems. One biographer, Ernest Jones, writes that for ten years, Freud suffered from a rather severe neurosis.

Jones points out that Freud had a monumental ego and was quite narcissistic. Among other interesting traits, the great psychoanalyst was alleged to have been a shameless moocher, borrowing extensively and perennially from friends, and even from his enemies, until well into middle age. Freud knew he was not a popular person, and he had a long succession of quarrels with friends and associates.

This is pointed out, not in an effort to discredit one of the great thinkers of our age, but to emphasize the universality of neurotic strivings.

Let's take a look at some of the manifestations of the inferiority complex and see how it works.

THE FIRST WITH THE WORST

The Hypercritical Person: Will Durant once said that to speak ill of others is a dishonest way of praising ourselves. This is precisely what we do when we become critical. By proclaiming the faults of others, we appear to be saying that we are superior. The worst critic is the one who suffers the most from an inferiority complex.

A close relative of the harsh critic is the gossip monger, who is always "the first with the worst." By disseminating rumors and gossip, he or she is quietly taking joy in the discomfiture or weaknesses of others. Then there is a secondary gain. While relaying some bit of scandal or misfortune, the gossip monger is in the spotlight and is thus the focus of attention. This is one of the chief goals of such persons. One cynical purveyor of bad news said to a friend, "I never say anything about a person unless it's something good, and boy, is this *good!*"

Gossip is a form of character assassination as well as an attention-getting device.

How Can We Measure Success?

Status seeking is another very common form of proclaiming our sense of inferiority. Everyone is tinged with some feelings of self-doubt, and even extremely gifted people have their islands of inferiority. It is axiomatic that grasping for symbols of status is a dead giveaway.

Francis de Sales once said, "Some men become proud and arrogant because they ride a fine horse, wear a feather in their hat or are dressed in a fine suit of clothes. Who does not see the folly of this? If there be any glory in such things, the glory belongs to the horse, the bird, or the tailor."

People with total self-acceptance and no trace of inferiority feelings (and they would be rare) would never be concerned with impressing others with their brilliance, possessions, or achievements. Some wit has said that most people spend money they don't have on things they don't need to impress people they don't like.

One difficulty is that there are relatively few ways of measuring success except through our achievements or possessions. If you have a tendency toward a preoccupation with status—a mark of inferiority feelings—don't be too hard on yourself. Until we have conquered our self-doubts and proven to ourselves that we are indeed worthwhile persons, we may well need some props for our sagging egos.

Great achievers, as well as men and women of great wealth and social prestige, often gain enormous satisfaction from seeing their pictures in the press or their names linked with even more famous persons. Social leaders, intellectual giants, and tycoons are usually tinctured with this sense of insecurity and inferiority. We seldom lose our need for acceptance, approval, and affection.

NOT GOOD ENOUGH

Freud has pointed out that it is difficult if not impossible to distinguish between guilt and inferiority. We can actually link together inferiority, guilt, shame, failure, and poverty—for these are just different words to describe the generalized feeling that repeats over and over the doleful refrain, "I'm not good enough; love me, notice me, affirm me."

The obsessive-compulsive personality always has some feeling of inadequacy or inferiority. Remembering that nearly all excessiveness—that is, all neurosis—originates in childhood, we can see how the compulsive person has come by his neurosis legitimately. Emotions have no chronology. There is no diminishing of childhood feelings of shame, guilt, or inferiority. They remain embedded in the adult personality unless or until they are exorcised by intensive therapy such as Primal Integration.

The compulsive eater, drinker, talker, or worker is a good example. Consider first the compulsive eater. Such a person eats in order to tranquilize some inner anxiety. Food becomes a substitute for love. The compulsive eater did not receive sufficient love in a form he or she could accept.

Take an extreme example, that of the person suffering from *anorexia nervosa.* Several young women have been treated at the Burlingame Counseling Center for this ailment. Most are between the ages of eighteen and twenty-six. They starve themselves, or eat and then induce vomiting because they perceive themselves as overweight. A certain proportion starve themselves to death.

A typical case was a young woman who came to us suffering from a combination of anorexia and bulimia. She would go on eating binges, consuming enormous quantities of food and then in shame and revulsion proceed to starve herself. Life became a daily struggle between the urge to eat and the equally strong compulsion to starve herself.

She understood the origin, but insight seldom cures. Her father had urged her, when she was quite small, to "eat a lot and be big and strong." All his relatives were overweight. Her mother urged her to diet and lose weight. Thus, as a small child, she was constantly torn between the two authoritarian voices: eat; diet; get big and strong; lose weight and be slender.

In her primal sessions, she did more than remember the double messages she had received from her parents. She relived those scenes, hearing the voices and admonitions with as much clarity and intensity as when she was a small girl. She now has the compulsion under control.

Her compulsive behavior was rooted in feelings of inadequacy. She felt a failure because she could never please her parents. The conflicting messages made it impossible for her to succeed. Hence, she ended with strong feelings of self-rejection, despite a good mind, a friendly personality, and numerous other positive attributes.

For dessert one night, another young woman ate a candy bar, two bags of cookies, an eclair, three sandwiches, crackers and dip, a jar of peanut butter and half a jar of jelly, raisins and berries, two slices of bread with cheese and mayonnaise, a large pizza, and four bowls of cereal. Then she made herself throw up.

Such eating binges and self-induced vomiting, termed bulimia, or *bulimia-nervosa*, usually affect young women and often begin in adolescence or the late teens.

This is their way of handling the stress caused by factors of which they are almost always unaware. As many as 20 percent of college women experience this binge-purge problem to some degree, according to Dr. Craig Johnson of the Anorexia Nervosa Center at Chicago's Michael Reese Hospital and Medical Center.

Only by reliving the repressed childhood experiences which precipitated the symptoms are bulimarectics enabled to overcome this problem.

> Almost all those afflicted are women—also true of the better-known eating disorder *anorexia nervosa*, the "starvation disease." . . . Anorectics are mostly shy, withdrawn females who develop their symptoms around the onset of puberty. Bulimarectics tend to be extroverted, successful perfectionists who start the gorging behavior in their late teens, and often have trouble seeing their problem as more than an idiosyncrasy—one reason why it is so little known to the public. Anorectics are cadaverously thin, while bulimarectics generally weigh in at normal levels.[1]

"LISTEN TO ME! HEAR ME!"

The compulsive talker deserves special attention. The overtalkative are usually very miserable. They are able to relieve their inner tension only by incessant talking. If they didn't talk nonstop, they would then feel their anxiety.

This compulsiveness is rooted in primal pain. The details would vary, but in essence very talkative people did not receive sufficient love and affirmation as children. They may have been loved, but not in a form they could accept. In some instances, a loving mother and a critical father can produce the same results—or an unloving mother and an adoring father. The incessant, irritating verbalizing of compulsive people is a discharge of anxiety, through focusing attention on themselves.

Because of a weak ego structure, the overtalkers need to reassure themselves that they are being heard; that people are listening. It never occurs to wordy people that they are dominating the conversation. Such people *need* to talk, just as the alcoholic needs a drink to allay the anxiety generated by feelings of insecurity and inferiority.

A common manifestation of the inferiority complex is a tendency toward *extreme self-consciousness.* Uninformed people sometimes pronounce these people self-centered. They are actually centered on their own pain, originating in childhood feelings of inadequacy.

It is not uncommon to observe great differences in children from the same family. One may be outgoing and gregarious, while another is quiet, shy, withdrawn, and self-conscious. The latter usually has great difficulty learning the art of small talk. Such people are seldom good conversationalists, because they did not develop adequate social skills. Overly self-conscious people have deep feelings of inferiority. They may be greatly endowed with intelligence, and significant talents, but if they as children were not affirmed in an acceptable manner, they grow up feeling inferior in social situations.

Inferiority feelings reveal themselves both in nonstop talkers and in silent people who feel too self-conscious to express themselves.

Another aspect of inferiority needs to be mentioned. Insecure people with self-doubts are usually extremely *sensitive.* Only people with total self-acceptance would be unaffected by criticism. They would have such a strong sense of self-worth that criticism would bother them no more than the comment of a four-year-old child saying petulantly, "I don't like you." Unfortunately, only a very small percentage of the population experiences total self-acceptance. The rest of us are marred in some degree.

Most of us would rather be ruined by fatuous praise than saved by honest criticism. This is the measure of our almost universal lack of proper self-esteem.

REPETITION AND ANXIETY

Another fairly common symptom of the obsessive-compulsive-phobic personality is seen in the person who feels the urge to carry out certain *repetitive acts* whether they make any sense or not. Psychiatrist William Sargant has pointed out that the great Samuel Johnson had to touch certain posts when he walked down Fleet Street in London. Some of these little obsessive acts are harmless, unless they spread to so many areas of one's life as to interfere with productive living. Dr. Sargant writes:

> An Oxford professor of the twenties anxiously asked the late Dr. William Brown whether his compulsion always to walk up and down the room when he lectured, in sequence of seven steps, was dangerous. Brown, with his tongue in cheek put his mind at rest: "When you find yourself walking in multiples of seven, come to see me again! Simple sevens are all right." There are, indeed, progressive degrees of obsession.
>
> A mother, for instance, may worry continually that she may have dropped an open safety pin in a milk bottle, and the bottle will be returned to the dairy but not washed properly, and the next child who drinks from this bottle will swallow the safety pin. She may be perfectly aware of the wildly improbable nature of this repetitive fear, but nevertheless, feels compelled to examine every empty milk

bottle five or six times before the milk man collects it. In all other respects, she may be a sensible and efficient housewife. Others, with minor symptoms of the same illness, make sure before going to bed that all gas taps are turned off and all doors properly locked. They rationalize their behavior by saying, "All sensible people make several security checks; it is worth the trouble."[2]

The Work Addict

Then there are the workaholics. Dedicated, compulsive workers usually have some of these attributes: They work long hours, bring work home from the office, sometimes go back on Saturday to "clean up the desk," and seldom have time for their families, or vacations. They usually dislike taking vacations if they are true workaholics. If their spouses leave them, they rationalize that she or he was neurotic and needed an excessive amount of attention.

When challenged, they point out that they are doing it all for the family. They are not consciously lying; they sincerely believe this explanation. In reality, they are work-addicts. They work excessively for the same reason that alcoholics drink to excess, or food addicts overeat. They work excessively to keep their anxieties from surfacing. They say that they enjoy their work, and they do enjoy the fact that their addiction prevents them from experiencing a nameless fear that drives them constantly. Instead of choosing the liquor route, they find greater release from tensions by turning out vast amounts of work. Theirs is one of the few respectable neuroses, although it can be quite destructive to health, serenity, and relationships.

To understand compulsive workers, we need to use the word *introjection*. This term applies to the way in which children derive their conscience. Virtually all our *shoulds* and *oughts* originate in our early environment. Parental demands and expectations are introjected into children's minds. They absorb parental values and concepts. If father is a compulsive worker, one or more of the children will tend to follow his example. Being constantly busy becomes the requirement. It is *good* to be always in motion; it is *bad* to sit down and rest. Another child may make father a negative role model. Disliking Dad's incessant busyness, she makes a conscious decision to be just as different as possible.

A woman who came to our counseling center with a severe anxiety neurosis told us that her mother had been a rigid, demanding perfectionist whose hands were never idle. Barbara said, "I wanted to be as different from my mother as possible. I'm not sloppy, but I'm not a perfectionist either. I refuse to be." Yet she had a full-blown neurosis, a deep-seated anxiety, which had no particular focus. Having only a negative role model, in a sense Barbara had to invent her own personality. She had no positive pattern to go by, hence the severe anxiety that destroyed her marriage and her peace of mind.

Compulsive workers must be constantly busy in order to mute the sound of that parent tape that keeps demanding, "Keep busy; don't sit down; you're lazy; have you finished your homework? Work first, then play! You'll never amount to anything." They must keep busy in response to that incessant tape running constantly in their heads, and to prove to their parent (in their own heads) and to themselves that they *do* amount to something. Besides, society rewards the achiever: "I don't see how you accomplish so much; you're the busiest person I know." They must never sink below the expectations of the demanding parent or of their own inner judicial system.

Workaholics experience generalized anxiety, which may be rooted in repressed fear, anger, inferiority, or guilt. They are not aware of these emotions. They simply feel anxious and tense when they aren't busy. Inactivity permits the anxiety to surface. They can suppress it only by being super-industrious. Thus they hold down the pain—pain originating in childhood traumas or simply the lack of love.

On the other hand, there are people who genuinely enjoy their work, who are called workaholics, yet they are able to take vacations, seldom bring their work home, and simply derive great satisfaction from their jobs.

A woman who felt driven to be constantly busy said that her mother urged her to read, but when she found her reading, would urge her to get busy with the housework. "I got a double message," she said, "but the overriding one was that I should be constantly busy. As an adult, I felt driven to find work to do. I feel guilty if I sit down for a few minutes to read." Thus are our neuroses created.

Everything Done Perfectly

Another kind of compulsiveness is shown in *perfectionists*. Such people may be lint pickers, picture straighteners, neatniks, compulsively clean and tidy. They will usually feel anxious if there are any evidences of the slightest imperfection around them.

I counseled with a couple who illustrated the tendency of the perfectionist to marry a more relaxed person. Ben was a technically minded individual. His wife was much more relaxed. Ben had unconsciously sought a wife with spontaneity. She had been drawn to someone who was more organized than she.

Ben became upset over what he called his wife's sloppiness. She in turn became angry over his neurotic complaints.

Ben was raised in an orphanage where little love was shown. In a desperate need to win attention and love, he became compulsively neat and organized. Now as an adult, a displaced household article made him furious. He kept his primal pain down only by seeing to it that everything was done perfectly, at work and in his home.

It should be added that Ben also had difficulty with his business associates. Only after extensive counseling was Ben able to relax some of his neurotic perfectionism.

A woman related this incident: She was affixing a stamp to a letter and her husband said with considerable concern, "No, no, not that way. Look. . . ." He took the stamp and envelope and said, "It should be put on *this* way." He then showed her that the stamp should be placed with *precisely* the same amount of space showing at the top and right hand side. Her casually putting the stamp at approximately in the right place generated anxiety in him. This could be labeled an anxiety neurosis, a compulsion, a feeling of guilt or shame unless things are done with absolute perfection.

ALIENATION FROM THE "PERFECT" FAMILY

It is not necessarily the slum-dwelling family that produces the deepest sense of self-rejection. Blaine Goodrich, writing in the *Washington Post*, has pointed out that in many wealthy suburbs, privileged children and young people are growing up with a deep sense of *alienation from self, parents, and society.*

> The daughter of a wealthy real estate developer drove her mother's sports car out to a park . . . and hanged herself from a tree.
>
> The 24-year-old son of a prominent chemistry professor . . . entered his parents' spacious home with a knife. This bright but aimless young man whom friends said was always dwarfed by the brilliance of his father, stabbed [his father] in the heart as he lay asleep.[3]

The author documents his story with many similar instances of children of wealth who fail to develop a normal sense of self-worth.

Harvard sociologist David Reisman, author of *The Lonely Crowd*, points out that this is a fairly common problem, and indicates that John Hinckley, the accused assailant of President Reagan, fits the pattern of young men from successful families who are overshadowed by the achievements of their siblings or parents and wander off into their own private world.[4]

Psychiatrist Alexander Lowen describes a related form of compulsive behavior:

> The illusion of being a perfect mother demands a "perfect child" and leads to the rejection of the . . . child, who needs his mother's understanding and support. The perfect mother becomes a desperate and destructive woman.
>
> The desperate person reacts to every situation as if it were "a matter of life or death." Every issue poses the question of survival. Every problem is viewed as a choice between black and white. Each decision is burdened by the alternatives of all or nothing. The result is that the desperate person gets nothing; he manages to survive, but fails to satisfy any of his wishes. Freud pointed out that the neurotic ignores reality, while the psychotic denies it.[5]

SPIRITUAL PERFECTION

One aspect of perfectionism is related to the neurotic drive for spiritual perfection. There is obviously nothing wrong with setting our goals high and trying to achieve the highest possible degree of spiritual growth, but again we are forced to consider our definition of neurosis: "excessiveness." The striver after spiritual perfection can develop such neurotic symptoms as *scrupulosity*. This is often found among people who have chosen to focus on spiritual growth to the exclusion of all else. They become obsessed with minutiae. The slightest deviation from perfection drives them into orgies of confession. They become guilt-ridden, obsessed with trivialities, often convinced that they may have committed the unpardonable sin.

A Roman Catholic priest once said that listening to the confessions of nuns was like being stoned to death with popcorn.

When we are blind to some great sin, such as pride, arrogance, or lust, we tend to confess some lesser sin all the more vehemently. Frequently, the greater moral failure is buried in the unconscious mind and must be dredged up with intensive therapy.

CAN OBSESSIONS BE CURED?

William Sargant states that some people with obsessional neurosis have gone for treatment for as long as fifteen years without being cured. However, it has now been demonstrated that obsessive-compulsive-phobic neurosis, or virtually any other neurotic behavior pattern can be cured by Primal Integration therapy.

Sargant points out in his book, written before Primal Integration had been discovered as the cure for neurosis:

> Some patients are clearly helped toward recovery when forgotten memories are brought to consciousness. Both Freud and Pavlov . . . suggest that repressed emotional incidents may create severe generalized anxiety in some temperamental types. . . . This provides a physiological basis for Freud's observation that repressed emotional memories often lead to a condition of chronic anxiety about apparently unconnected matters. The . . . conditions may also disappear when the repressed memory is restored to

consciousness. . . . Intellectual indoctrination without emotional excitement is remarkably ineffective, as the empty pews of most English churches prove.[6]

We all need some kind of yardstick, or standard, by which to measure the degree of our performance. In the Olympics, for instance, there are world records for each event that contestants hope to equal or exceed. In the area of spiritual and emotional growth, we also need a scale to assist us in determining our performance and the areas in which we need to grow. If growth is the meaning of life, as I believe it is, then it is very important to determine the degree of our deficiencies and discover ways of overcoming those limitations.

Virtually everyone suffers to some degree from many of the following limitations. We need not feel discouraged if we fall into a substantial number of these categories. The important thing is to ascertain if our lives or performances are being limited by some of these negative personality traits.

Self-esteem is normally derived from parents and other authority figures who comprise the major portion of our early environment. Those who did not receive adequate love and affirmation in this way must then acquire a proper sense of self-worth by their own efforts. It is important to remember that we are not responsible for the way we are, but we *are* responsible (from here on out) for our own growth. To accomplish this, it is important to diagnose the problem and its intensity. In another chapter I will deal with steps that can be taken to reduce feelings of inferiority and achieve a greater degree of self-acceptance.

The degree of self-esteem varies from person to person. We can measure the need for growth by going over the following checklist. Remembering that the key word is *excessive*, read the list of personality traits and see how you rate:

	NONE	MILD	STRONG	SEVERE
		(check each trait)		
Timidity	—	—	—	—
Withdrawal tendencies	—	—	—	—
Antisocial behavior	—	—	—	—
A critical nature	—	—	—	—
Difficulty in communicating	—	—	—	—
Inablity to accept compliments easily	—	—	—	—
Dependency feelings	—	—	—	—
Alcohol or drug addiction	—	—	—	—
Hostility	—	—	—	—
Inferiority feelings	—	—	—	—
Passivity	—	—	—	—
Oversensitivity	—	—	—	—
Feelings of being unloved	—	—	—	—
Phobias	—	—	—	—
Compulsiveness	—	—	—	—
Obsessive thinking	—	—	—	—
Severe guilt feelings	—	—	—	—
Anxiety	—	—	—	—
Insomnia	—	—	—	—
Irrational anger	—	—	—	—
Jealousy	—	—	—	—
Guilt	—	—	—	—

CHAPTER FOUR

Power, Pride, and Inferiority

The lust of power is not rooted in strength, but in weakness.

Erich Fromm

Is there such a thing as a superiority complex? The usual answer is that what sometimes appears so is only an inferiority complex whistling in the dark.

Though they are rare, I have known a few people afflicted with this complex. In each case, there was an unwarranted amount of praise heaped upon the person in childhood. I once observed a superiority complex in the making.

THE SUPERIORITY COMPLEX

My wife and I were taking a trip up the Rhine. Seated near us on the deck were a father and son. The boy was about twelve. The father engaged us in conversation and began to tell us with vast enthusiasm about his son's marvelous mental abilities, while the boy sat soaking up the adulation. The description of his son's wonderful attributes consumed the better part of an hour.

When we chanced to be near them again, the father continued to sing the boy's praises. He was a whiz in school, a world beater in math and history with an enormously high IQ, good in sports, gracious and courteous to his elders, and popular with his classmates. On and on it went ad nauseum. The poor boy's sickening smugness foretold the kind of an adult he would almost certainly grow up to be—an insufferable snob who would have to learn the hard way that life deals harshly with those who think too highly of themselves.

My friend Bert was an only child, a straight-A student for whom great success had been prophesied by parents, relatives, and classmates. At the outset of his career, there were some fairly spectacular successes. He possessed a charming personality and appeared to be a good administrator. However, there were one or two rather significant flaws in his personality. The praise and adulation lavished upon him by his parents and others had given him a somewhat exalted opinion of himself, and he had difficulty bowing to the orders of his superiors. He couldn't make compromises and seemed harsh and unyielding in many instances. This unfortunate trait resulted in the breakup of his marriage and the end of several promising business ventures. His opinion of himself was out of proportion to his abilities.

Knowing him well, I would say that he was not covering up a weak self-esteem, but that he had that rare thing—a genuine superiority complex.

I have known several other men and women who were overpraised by their foolish parents. Though some were undoubtedly high achievers, in each instance they had personality traits that made them seem somewhat disagreeable. When later they discover that good looks or a high IQ alone do not bring success in life, most of them become sadly disillusioned. This prince or princess syndrome is painful, for there is always a time when those who experience it are dethroned.

THE ALL-POWERFUL INFANT

Egotism, conceit, arrogance all begin in infancy, with what is called infantile megalomania—small children feeling that they are in total control. Actually, they are. They are running things. The whole household is geared to meet their needs. They cry, and Mother comes running. They are hungry, and someone is there to give them their bottles. They smile, and parents rush for the camera. Friends and relatives ooh and ahh over them. Don't think for a moment that they are unaware of the adulation they are inspiring. They are the center of their universe and loving every minute of it. They're running the whole operation. They're all-powerful.

It is not difficult to surmise what infants must feel, being held in Mother's loving embrace and receiving unconditional love. It requires no flight of imagination to sense what they feel. They don't have to do anything to merit Mother's love. As precious darlings, they are fed, nurtured, admired, catered to, and given unlimited quantities of unconditional love. They don't have to earn it.

We know precisely what the infant experiences, for in many primal sessions we have heard and observed the re-experiencing of this infant euphoria. *Rapture* is the only word that can describe the initial feeling experienced by the infant.

This unearned rapture, this blissful euphoria, is like the Eden in which Adam and Eve first lived. But when this unconditional love is withdrawn, and little bundles of joy learn that they will have to earn Mother's approving smile, the rapture begins to diminish. As they learn that they cannot have every wish granted—for instance, having to go potty, cannot touch this or that, and required to do scores of things they really had no intention of doing—they are understandably outraged, and their screams of frustration and rage are not pleasant to hear. They are being evicted from Paradise. Mother no longer grants every whim. There are slaps on the hand and an occasional frown. There are a thousand rules and hundreds of no-no's. They are, sad to relate, no longer in control.

On the first day at kindergarten or the nursery, when Mother leaves—surely forever—their wails are heart-breaking. Their yearning for the rapture of their infant days will never end.

YEARNING FOR DEPENDENCY

Sometimes we try to regain our Eden by abdicating responsibility. There lies latent within most of us a longing for some distant South Sea island, where we can live on breadfruit and bananas, lulled to sleep at night by the gentle breeze and murmuring waves. There is nothing wrong with such a fantasy, but it is well to remember that it is rooted in an unconscious yearning for the rapture we once experienced when we were blissfully dependent, being lovingly cared for and with no responsibilities.

A university professor related that his mother, who had long been a wheelchair victim, leaped from her chair when the house caught fire and fled from the house. The chair burned up in the fire. She continued to walk without assistance and never needed the wheelchair again. She unconsciously had been enjoying the euphoria of being cared for, as in infancy. She sincerely believed that she was helpless.

A hypochondriac told me in a counseling session that the only time he had ever received love was when he was ill.

"Now as an adult," he said, "I go to any lengths to get attention from doctors, nurses, friends, or family members.

The only time I really feel loved is when I am ill or in a hospital. I get sick quite frequently, and I know it is based on my deep need for the nurturing I received when I was sick as a kid."

Self-acceptance implies the necessity of realizing that there is some remnant of the child within each of us who longs for this ancient rapture. The compulsive gambler or worker, the alcoholic, the drug abuser, the Don Juan, the sexually promiscuous woman, the manipulator, the sweet seductive "frightened fawn in the forest," the muscle man on the beach, the overachiever, the miser, the saint, and the spiritual giant are all seeking in different ways to recapture, if only briefly, a moment of that rapture.

There is a certain similarity between the wheelchair victim, the man with the vast wealth who sought more, and the man who sought love by becoming ill. Each of us is in some way related to them. No one ever got *enough* love, of the right kind, and there is resident in us—conscious or otherwise—a longing to recapture the rapture of unconditional love without having to *earn* it.

Our staunch denials that this is so could prompt a psychologist to say, "Methinks he doth protest too much." It would probably be more appropriate to recognize this in ourselves and to view ourselves with amused, friendly tolerance.

Unfortunately, we cannot live in a constant state of euphoria. Happiness is limited to rare moments in a lifetime, and we must settle for contentment, with occasional brief moments of true happiness.

Substitutes for the Rapture

Since we cannot regain our Edenic experience, we are driven to seek substitutes. Our struggle to achieve significantly is an echo of the primordial longing for the bliss of mother's unearned love. Whether it be praise, recognition, fame, wealth, badges, degrees, plaques, medals or certificates of merit, compliments, or even notoriety for which we struggle, the motivating power behind our search is the drive for the wonderful feeling of the rapture we once knew.

One of the world's richest men, when he was young, was told by his father that he would never amount to anything. Stung by the criticism he set out to prove his father wrong. He made his first million, before there were income taxes, at age thirty. By forty, he was a multimillionaire and far wealthier than his father. This gave him so much satisfaction that he embarked on a career that made him the richest man in the world, though not the most beloved. He settled for the satisfaction it gave him to prove his father wrong and to have the envy of those with lesser wealth. He became so wrapped up in his pursuit that he had little or no time for his family. One of his sons, in addressing him, called him "Mister."

This is not an effort to deprecate prosperity or wealth. We live in a materialistic world, and there is nothing inherently wrong with owning property or being wealthy. The only difficulty with an all-out struggle to win fame, power, or wealth is that it can never enable us to recapture the bliss from which spring so many of our longings.

Paul, a highly successful stockbroker, received an endless amount of unconditional love from his mother. She adored him as long as she lived. Paul could do no wrong. It is rare that a child receives so much love. In Paul's case, it was overdone. He got too much lavish praise.

The result was that Paul always lit up like a neon light in the presence of women. They found him attractive and enjoyed his company. His wife had often commented on the way he sparkled upon entering a room where there were women. He had thought her comments entirely facetious. Actually, there was a considerable concern on her part because of his overreaction to the presence of women.

Paul's wife ultimately discovered that he had had a series of affairs during their marriage. The latest one, which precipitated the crisis, was with a next-door neighbor. During his wife's absence, Paul had invited the neighbor into his home and into their bedroom. This proved an understandable trauma for his wife, and it took her quite some time to recover.

In our counseling sessions, it became obvious to me that Paul could never entirely overcome the sense of euphoria he experienced in the presence of women. He was a love addict.

Fortunately, he was sincere in his endeavor to get his neurosis under control and work out a successful marriage relationship. In our sessions together, he displayed a commendable honesty and openness in discussing his problem. He had a sincere desire to act appropriately, though he was aware that the old tendency would probably always be there. At last report, the marriage was on firm ground, and Paul had his obsession under control. He had been unconsciously seeking to recapture the rapture of unconditional love and adoration.

There is a legitimate God-given joy in being fulfilled. Aristotle called it entelechy, the divine growth principle, the built-in instinct for development, the drive to fulfill our highest destiny. It resides in all of life—whether a blade of grass, a tree, an animal, or a human being. It is the innate drive to accomplish a goal, to become one's best. It is only when the drive for attainment becomes excessive that we label it neurotic.

For instance, a friend told me of a relative who had married and divorced the same man four times. After each divorce, he would woo her, then she would experience again the bliss of romance and the glorious feeling of being in love again. As soon as they settled down to the daily routine of a normal married life, she would become morose and in time would divorce him. She was a romance addict.

THE UNIVERSAL LUST FOR POWER

The lust for power, originating in infancy and early childhood, takes many forms. The child's fascination with Superman and Flash Gordon is generated by the universal longing to be omnipotent. The person who passionately pursues the goal of popularity, power, adulation, wealth, or fame is in most instances simply compensating for some degree of insecurity or inferiority.

The tycoon with his millions, striving diligently for more, is not after money as such, but what it represents—power. The young motorcyclist roaring by on his souped-up motorcycle would not be nearly so happy if the noise level were reduced significantly, and his speed by half. He derives a sense of authority by gaining attention, even if it is disgust from people whose eardrums are being assaulted.

The enticing woman, seductively working on her next conquest, is not after love but power, reassurance; the Don Juan is similarly obsessed with the neurotic need to conquer women.

It is interesting that the first temptation recorded in Genesis has to do with power. Satan, in the guise of the serpent, informed Adam and Eve that if they would just sample a little of the fruit of the forbidden tree ("Don't touch that!" is mother's corresponding warning), they would be as gods—that is, all-powerful. Thus began the lust for omnipotence in the hearts of the first man and woman.

When Satan set out to tempt Jesus in the wilderness, he promised him world rule. Showing him all the kingdoms of the earth, Satan said, "All these will I give you if you will fall down and worship me" (Matthew 4:9). Here again is the appeal to the fundamental human lust for power. Jesus rebuked Satan, for as he said later, "My kingdom is not of this world" (John 18:36). This temptation was at the beginning of his ministry. At the very end, in his last appearance before his disciples, Jesus said, "All authority in heaven and on earth has been given to me" (Matthew 28:18). He could not settle for the title of world ruler, for his destiny was to be ruler of both heaven and earth.

Shakespeare recognized this universal lust for power:

> Man, proud man
> Drest in a little brief authority,
> Most ignorant of what he's most assured . . .
> Plays fantastic tricks before high heaven
> As makes the angels weep![1]

SELF-ADULATION

Power, praise, popularity, affirmation, acceptance, approval—how deeply ingrained is the lust for these evidences of our worth. The wife of a well-known Senator was quoted as saying, "I have talent. I got straight As in graduate school. I've still got my good looks. I know I've got all these terrific things going for me. I mean, my God, you are talking to, I think, one of the most fascinating women in this country."

John Lennon, at the peak of the Beatles' popularity, suggested that they were more popular than Jesus Christ; and Mohammed Ali referred to himself as the greatest man in history. Dr. John Schinel, director of the William A. White Institute of Psychiatry, points out that boasting is a

way of denying one's sense of insecurity. Andy Warhol once
said that in the future, everyone will be famous for fifteen
minutes, which would be a possible solution for the
popularity craze.

Among many similar ads in the Bay Area *Guardian* was
this:

> I am seeking a caring relationship with a non-smoking,
> very attractive, extremely sensual, highly intelligent, quite
> independent, well-proportioned, high energy woman under
> 36 years of age (mental and physical) who has a strong sense
> of self, is able to laugh easily, and is free of traditional sexist
> expectations concerning her friend/lover. You are offered
> intellectual stimulation, mutual respect, open honesty,
> adequate "space," human closeness, growth reinforcement,
> emotional support, sexual gratification, ideological compa-
> tability, a wide range of fun activities (flying, sailing, etc.),
> and a very busy, high energy, well-educated, financially
> secure, 5' 10", 167 pounds, attractive, sensitive, intelligent,
> huggable, humorous, serious 44-year-old man.[2]

The egotistical stance is nothing new. The Apostle Paul
had heard rumors of it in the church at Rome, and he wrote
them, "I bid every one among you not to think of himself
more highly than he ought to think. . . . Do not be haughty,
but associate with the lowly, never be conceited" (Romans
12:3, 16). Unfortunately, as Paul undoubtedly discovered,
the conceited person is never aware of that conceit, nor is
the arrogant individual conscious of being haughty. These
are usually defenses people use to cover some inner
weakness too painful to face.

THE DRIVE OF A SUPERACHIEVER

The need to overachieve can be a deadly drive. Rosemary
Clooney, a popular singer in the 1950s, made a comeback

thirty years later, after eight years of psychotherapy and a lengthy stay in a psychiatric hospital.

After she began her new career she said, "It was a need to overachieve. I was always too busy pretending to be the strong one; superwife and supersinger. I don't have to do that anymore. . . . I don't have to have another hit to prove that I can sing. Now I just do the best I can and try to make it interesting for myself. . . . When I feel I can't handle it anymore, I don't feel driven to put up a front."[3]

The *Psychiatric Dictionary* defines ambition as "a defense against shame." This is not to disparage a normal aspiration to achieve a worthy goal. It does suggest that too strong an ambition to reach the top can be neurotic, and therefore destructive.

According to Oliver Wendell Holmes, "Fame usually comes to those who are thinking about something else." Too frantic a pursuit of success can be a heartbreaking, coronary-inducing game.

It may be a source of confusion to some people to learn that ambition is a defense against the shame of inferiority, but, as it has been written, the truth will make you free, but first it may make you miserable. The bare truth can sometimes be shattering.

GREATNESS AND HUMILITY

La Rochefoucauld once said, "Though there are plenty of people who aspire to be pious, no one yearns to be humble." No doubt this could be attributed to the fact that we humans find it very difficult to abandon our prideful pursuits. Yet people are never heard to confess that their worst sin is that of pride, for the proud of heart are never aware of their defect. They go to great pains to conceal this hideous truth from themselves.

Einstein the scientist has been honored by people of many nations, but Einstein the man of humility has been even more greatly honored. Those who knew him personally speak of his grace, his compassion without condescension, his lack of vanity, his sense of humor and love of beauty.

He stated he had no special gifts, only passionate curiosity. He insisted that the most profound emotion we humans can experience is the sense of the mystical, which he called the source of all true art and science. Religion, he said, consisted of what he termed the slightest details we are able to perceive with our frail and feeble minds.

CHAPTER FIVE

Guilt and Self-Esteem

This sense of guilt is dumb; it does not tell him he is guilty, he does not feel guilty, he simply feels ill. This sense of guilt expresses itself only as a resistance to recovery, which is extremely difficult to overcome.

Sigmund Freud

If we were brought to trial for the crimes we have committed against ourselves, few would escape the gallows.

Germaine St. Cloud

A young woman who had come from another country for Primal Integration relived hour after hour, day after day, the terrible experience of being sadistically abused by an older sister who was mentally retarded. The parents forbade Sharon to resist in any way or even to complain.

Sharon felt guilty over the understandable anger she felt toward her sister. As a result of her repressed hostility, she developed a severe case of psoriasis. This is normally considered incurable.

As is usual in most primal sessions, she first experienced hurt and humiliation, then fear, and finally anger. It came out at last in great bursts of honest rage as she relived her childhood. She wrote later:

Generally, I feel quite relaxed, that I am a person of worth, and relieved of carrying all the problems of the world on my shoulders. I feel now I would rather live than die. My

73

destructive feelings have been enormous. I no longer feel I am a victim of other people's opinion of me.

I function much better, especially in my work situation. Formerly, every mistake I made registered as a pain in the neck or elsewhere in my body. While I make about as many mistakes as before, I am not mistake conscious. I am even able to laugh at myself.

I can now live more in the present than in the past. I am still struggling to forgive a certain person, but this is something within the last two years, not something from thirty-five years ago.

My relationships are greatly improved, whereas they were very strained before. I am able to listen to my parents even if their stories are uninteresting, because I know they need someone to listen to them so they can feel their own worth. Before my Primal Integration therapy, I couldn't do this, because my hurts were too deep.

My skin condition is greatly improved. . . . A few weeks ago some friends said they couldn't get over how well I expressed myself. This was meaningful, because my pastor had told me that I had never been able to communicate. I bought that as gospel truth, but lately I have gotten quite a lot of compliments on my ability to communicate.

I have been able to forgive the people in my past completely—a big dividend.

She later reported that her skin disease was almost entirely cured. There were many other important dividends.

I found it extremely interesting that she did not mention the older sister who had caused her so much grief. To Sharon, it just didn't seem important now that all her hurt and anger were discharged.

Her false guilt over repressed anger had felt like real guilt—guilt over a real sin—and the mind had handed its conflict and pain over to the body in the form of psychosomatic symptoms.

REAL AND FALSE GUILT

Guilt is without doubt the most damaging of all emotions. When we become aware that we have violated ethical or moral principles, or failed to abide by our own convictions, there is a lessening of self-worth.

Real and false guilt are equally destructive, for a person's inner judicial system, where judgment takes place, cannot distinguish between the two. It knows only good and bad, black and white. Real guilt is defined as a violation of the laws of man or God. False guilt is the feeling one experiences when, having genuinely repented and received forgiveness, a person continues to confess the same sin over and over.

Another aspect of false guilt can be illustrated by a scene I witnessed at a retreat. The group members were all strangers to one another. As an ice-breaker the leader played some rather rousing music with a definite beat to it. He then asked the group to stand and move with the music. All participated except one young woman who sat stiffly in her chair. Someone reached out to her and invited her to participate. She said, "No, my religion forbids me to dance." Nothing that was being done could have been construed as dancing, but to her, even swaying with the music was a sin. Had she begun to move with the music she would have violated her own conscience and felt guilty, but since such action is not an actual violation of any moral or spiritual law, there could have been no real guilt. She would have suffered false guilt, which to her would have felt precisely the same as real guilt. Ben N. Ard, Jr., writes,

> The individual who blames himself for acting badly (or sometimes for even thinking about acting badly) will usually feel (as blamers usually do) that he should be punished for his poor behavior. His internalized verdict therefore will go

somewhat as follows: "I committed a horrible crime. I am therefore a terrible sinner and must atone for my sins, punish myself for this crime. But if I keep doing badly, there is the danger of getting caught. If I continue committing these kinds of crimes, I will certainly be caught or will have to keep being anxious about the danger of being caught. My being caught and punished will be a hard, punishing thing. Therefore, it would be better if I kept committing crimes like this in order to punish myself, and therefore, atone for my sins." The vicious circle is complete.[1]

Criminals who repeat their crimes are unconsciously hoping to be apprehended, in order to experience the relief of being able to atone for their misdeeds.

A merciful God forgives when we repent, and remembers our sins no more (Jeremiah 31:34), but our own inner judicial system is keeping score. If we were reared in a judgmental and punitive environment, the conscience becomes vindictive and accusatory, whether the "sin" has been real or imaginary.

For instance, Sharon felt guilty and sinful because she had so much anger toward her older sister. This was false guilt, but the inner judicial system accused and punished her just the same with a physical symptom.

GUILT, CONSCIENCE, AND GOD

A delightful man shared with me in a counseling session that he was having an affair with his secretary and had thought about leaving his wife, but after due consideration, felt he could not do so. However, he could not end the affair. He was obviously suffering intense conflict. I asked if he had a severe conscience, and he said, "Yes, I get the guilties easily."

I asked him if he had any accidents lately.

"Yes, I wrecked my car recently."

"Have you had any physical symptoms?"

"Yes, I have quite a bit of stomach trouble, incipient ulcers."

Everyone doesn't have the same kind of conscience, but those with an average to severely punitive judicial system will unconsciously find a way to punish themselves. They become accident-prone, sickness-prone or failure-prone —sometimes all three—depending upon the severity of the conscience.

Twenty-five hundred years ago, Plato wrote, "The guilty soul runs eagerly to its judge." He understood the tendency to punish ourselves for real or false guilt. Then dealing with the matter of physical ailments he added, "It is not the body that is sick, but the man." More than two thousand years before modern medicine discovered psychosomatic ailments, Plato announced this profound truth.

We humans normally find it much more difficult to forgive ourselves than God does, and it is usually easier for us to forgive another than ourselves, especially if we possess an overly sensitive conscience.

The inner judicial system does not deal solely in terms of sins and major crimes. It encompasses our every action. For instance, I get a feeling of virtue and self-approval when I am able to get my desk cleaned up, with every letter answered and each telephone call returned. But when my desk is cluttered with unfinished work, I feel "bad." As in a court of justice, there are only two verdicts available to the inner judicial system: guilty or innocent.

The Bible defines the sin of omission: "Whoever knows what is right to do and fails to do it, for him it is sin" (James 4:17). And sin (missing the mark) must be either forgiven or punished.

Our consciences are not created by God. They are made *available* to us by God as pure blank slates, upon which our parents and our peers, our teachers and preachers, and our culture in general write their code of moral and ethical behavior. When we violate our own personal code, we do not so much offend God as ourselves. As parents are alarmed when their small child disobeys and runs across a busy street, so God is deeply concerned when we act contrary to divine law and violate our consciences. God's concern, I am sure, is akin to that of the parents who are fearful that their child may be hit by a car and injured or killed. He is concerned lest we be hurt. In his love, he wants the best for us, and our best is to seek his will as our highest goal.

The word *concern* comes from the Latin *concernere,* meaning "to distinguish, to see thoroughly in the mind, to worry." I don't suggest that God worries, but I am certain that he is deeply concerned for us and our welfare.

GUILT AND ANGER

Anger is one of the strongest emotions given us by God. It can be very destructive at times, and many parents punish their children for being angry. Thus many people grow into adulthood feeling guilty about this emotion. It is especially true if parents punished the child severely for showing anger.

A man was told by his mother that he had been a very willful child, and at age five, he had thrown a tantrum in a store because she wouldn't buy some toy for him. She said, "I'd had enough of your tantrums, so I took you outside and spanked you with a piece of a shingle I always carried with me. After that you were a good boy."

The man, then in his fifties, said: "I didn't become a 'good boy.' My anger simply went underground. Thereafter, I never dared express the slightest displeasure to my parents, much less anger. To this day, I have difficulty getting in touch with my anger. I experience it chiefly in terms of psychosomatic symptoms, neckaches, arthritis, bursitis, and a generalized inner tension that never leaves me."

It may seem strange that a child who is punished for a single tantrum retains the message that all anger is forbidden, but that is the way some children react to punishments.

Those who are not subject to psychosomatic symptoms, yet repress their anger, often discover that the guilt over having denied this emotion will reveal itself in some other way: by causing the person to become accident- or failure-prone. The judge—the internal system—will find a way to punish the guilty person. It is not God who punishes but the inner self.

It is my contention that God does not punish, but when we violate some divine law or our own conscience, the inner judicial system finds a way to do the punishing. In a sense, there are neither rewards nor punishments, only consequences—and often they may seem like punishment, and in a sense, they are—but it is not God who does the punishing. We simply violate divine laws to our own destruction. There are consequences for everything in this life. Each bit of goodness has its positive results, and each deviation from righteousness will have its negative consequences. Whether God or the inner self does the condemning makes very little difference; the sentence is carried out inexorably.

Is it wrong to be angry? Richard P. Walters points out that there are 365 references to God's anger in the Old Testament, as well as 80 references to human anger. "The Hebrew word for anger that is used most frequently is *aph*, which translates literally as *nostril*. This idea of snorting out anger is attributed 177 times to God and 45 times to man. . . . Because God is divine, his anger is a natural expression and reaction to man's unholiness and ungodliness. Yet, God's wrath is only one part of his character and is usually closely related to his love and compassion. God also describes himself as slow to anger."[2]

IT'S OKAY TO GET ANGRY AT GOD

The great sin for many people would be to get angry at God. Yet, there are numerous instances of biblical characters doing so. Jews had no difficulty having a confrontation with God. Job, for instance, felt considerable irritation and possibly anger at God, for his terrible suffering: "I cry out to you, O God, but you do not answer; I stand up, but you merely look at me. You turn on me ruthlessly, with the might of your hand you attack me" (30:20-21). Job is called a perfect man by God, and there is no evidence that God rebuked him for his outburst.

David, whom the Bible calls a man after God's own heart, became quite angry on occasion. We love his beautiful poems of praise, but little attention is paid to the imprecatory psalms, in which he is very hostile and complains about God's treatment of him. In Psalms 10, 13, 22, 31, 60, 88, and especially in Psalm 109, the writer is very angry. Sometimes indignation is expressed toward God; at other times it is directed toward the psalmist's enemies. We are all familiar with the beautiful Twenty-third Psalm, but in the twenty-second, also attributed to David, we read: "My God, my God, why hast thou forsaken me? Why art thou so far from helping me? . . . O my God, I cry by day, but thou dost not answer; and by night, but find no rest" (vv. 1-2).

Yet even in the irate psalms, there is more praise than lament, more faith than doubt, more trust than despair. With rare exception, the hostile psalms end on a note of praise and understanding, as though, having expressed all his complaints and anger, the psalmist could now thank and praise God.

This is good religion and good therapy. Don't be afraid to tell God precisely how you feel. He knows anyway, so you might just as well tell him. But do it with *feeling*. This is no time for false piety and a stained-glass window voice and King James terminology. If you are angry at him, tell him so! When you sense in some corner of your soul that you actually hate God, tell him so. His reaction, I am sure, is like that of a father whose angry four-year-old child screams at her daddy, "I hate you!" and dashes for her room to let out a burst of frustration. The loving daddy will tiptoe into her room a bit later, when the storm clouds have lifted, and say something like, "I understand how you feel, honey. You're upset because Daddy won't let you have something you want very much. But it's okay to get mad at me. When I was little, I got mad at my mommy and daddy, too. I understand. Daddy loves you."

Isaiah, that masterful prophet, had no hesitation about accusing God and telling him precisely how he felt, "Truly you are a God who hidest himself, O God and Savior of Israel" (45:15 NIV).

On one occasion, Elijah felt so alone, frightened, and helpless that he asked to die. He experienced a whole gamut of emotions, but one could sum them up by saying that he felt inferior, inadequate, and defeated. Instead of rebuking him, God gently urged him to compose himself and get back to work.

When Jonah suffered the ignominy of being swallowed and then vomited up by a great fish, he prophesied the destruction of Nineveh at divine command, then grew very angry with God because the city was not destroyed. He *wanted* it wiped out, despite their repentance. God dealt very gently with him in his frustration and anger, as tenderly as a loving mother with a grossly irritated child.

I am convinced that God is kinder and more loving than we give him credit for. "His steadfast love endures forever" (Psalm 107:1). All he asks is that we seek to obey his beautiful, divine, beneficent will. So, if you are frustrated with God, let him know and don't spare the harsh words. Be honest. There is no guilt in being angry.

HOW TO HANDLE ANGER

Unexpressed anger goes underground. Those who grew up in homes where negative emotions were forbidden are often totally unaware that they are resentful. The repressed hurt and indignation may express itself in various ways: depression, anxiety, rheumatoid arthritis, migraine headaches, gastrointestinal problems, severe psoriasis, and eczema. Inert material can be swept under the rug, but emotions are not lifeless. They are active, dynamic expressions of the emotional structure. If denied outward expression, they will always find a way to manifest themselves.

We need to distinguish between *repression,* which means the total denial of an emotion, and *suppression,* which suggests awareness of a feeling held in check.

Thus one has three alternatives: we may unconsciously *repress* the emotion, *suppress* it for whatever reason, or *express* it if it seems appropriate. It is repression—denial—which causes the most damage to one's personality, but to suppress powerful emotions (anger at an employer, for instance) can also be destructive. One might appropriately hold the anger in temporarily and then express it to a friend, in order to discharge the force of the emotion. Bottled up anger is usually destructive, physically or emotionally.

We have no right, however, to dump our anger on some unsuspecting person. There is no justification for robbing someone of peace of mind just because we want to vent our indignation. We have a right to let someone know how we feel, but not a license to destroy that person and ruin our relationship. Some better alternatives:

1. Tell a sympathetic listener, and thus discharge the pent-up emotional intensity.
2. Write a letter outlining the grievances, justifying yourself in every way possible. But *don't mail the letter.* I have often used the letter-writing solution, and whenever I have foolishly mailed it, I have always regretted it afterwards.
3. Go to your room and close the door. Then pound on the bed and kick it, yell, and excoriate the evil doer. Don't bother to sound nice and polite. Use any language that seems appropriate to the situation.
4. Tell God how badly you have been misused. Call on him to punish the destroyer of your peace of mind. Read the 109th Psalm and get permission right out of the Bible to sound mean, hostile, and vengeful.

When anger is spent, you will be able to think more rationally and act with logic more than with emotion. You may even find yourself praising God, as the psalmist did so often after getting a load of hostility out of his system.

Guilt Brings Loss of Self-Esteem

But we humans feel guilty about more things than anger. There is a vast category of sins to which the flesh is heir, and every time we violate the laws of God, man, or our own judicial system, we feel—or should feel—guilty. Since, as has been noted previously, it is virtually impossible to distinguish between guilt and inferiority, in letting guilt reside unresolved within us, we begin to feel less worthy and more inferior. There is a loss of self-esteem when we are guilty, for before the tribunal of our own souls we have pronounced ourselves unworthy.

Feeling guilty, a passive person often indulges in self-condemnation. The aggressive individual with a poor self-image will usually, as we have seen, find it extremely difficult to admit any error or weakness. Such a person must be right at all costs.

A prominent business man once said to me, "I was forty years old before I could say, 'I don't know,' or 'I was wrong.' " It takes strength and humility to admit our weaknesses.

GUILT AND FEAR

When you are driving sixty-five miles an hour in a fifty-five m.p.h. zone and suddenly hear the wail of a police siren, you become aware of a sudden emotion. It is not guilt you feel, but fear of being apprehended, plus having to sit there in the car while the grim-faced policeman asks for your license, and other drivers pass by, glancing at you with a mixture of amusement or gratification that it is you and not they.

You may be guilty, but the emotion is one of fear of punishment, or exposure. But if, perchance, the police car passes you and flags down a speeding vehicle just in front of you, you feel relief. You are still guilty of having broken the law, yet you feel only relief, a sense of pleasure that you were not caught.

We often confuse the emotions of guilt and fear. Consider the feeling you would experience if every wicked thought and each wrong deed you have committed throughout your life were suddenly flashed upon a gigantic outdooroutdoor screen near where you live or work. Perhaps there would be a whole galaxy of feelings—shame, embarrassment, guilt, and fear—but the predominant emotion is one of fear over having to face the friends and associates who have seen the horrifying disclosure of your innermost secrets. (If it wouldn't bother you in the slightest, then you are devoid of the slightest trace of a decent conscience or have lived a life of utter perfection.)

Most Christians are familiar with the biblical statement, "Perfect love casts out fear," but that is only part of the verse. Read on: "There is no fear in love, but perfect love casts out fear. For *fear has to do with punishment*" (I John 4:18).

So here, in a letter written two thousand years ago, is the basic truth about guilt and fear: Fear at its core originates in the small child's fear of punishment and continues to reside in the adult in its many manifestations.

GUILT, CONFLICT, AND ANXIETY

It is recorded that when Charles Darwin returned from his renowned voyage to the South Seas, he was certain he was suffering from a serious heart disease. His diary reveals his symptomatic attacks occurred when he was experiencing severe anxiety. Among other symptoms, he suffered from such excessive fatigue that he was unable to attend to daily obligations. A professor at the London School of Hygiene and Tropical Medicine, A. W. Woodruff, ventured the opinion that Darwin's physical symptoms were the result of inner conflict and perhaps a sense of guilt toward his father, who had wanted him to enter the ministry. Darwin was about to announce his theory of organic evolution and sensed it would arouse a vast deal of controversy, and most certainly criticism from his father. In a letter to a friend,

Darwin stated that announcing his scientific discovery was tantamount to confessing to murder.

Much of our anxiety is rooted in the fear of disapproval we felt as children, when we faced the loss of parental love. This primal fear of rejection is retained in the adult organism and is experienced as anxiety and tension.

The words *anxious, anguish,* and *anxiety* come from the Latin *angere,* to choke. Thus when we choke back anger, we experience anxiety, with resulting tension.

Guilt produces conflict, which causes anxiety, which in turn results in physical tension. In a study made at the Mayo Clinic, 562 patients who complained of pain in some part of the body were examined. "Intensive physical evaluations revealed no organic basis for the pain. The investigators reaffirmed the . . . observation that, for many, anxiety is replaced by a symptom such as pain. Many people with sexual conflicts prefer to talk to their physicians about physical symptoms rather than face the fact that they are anxious."[3]

The effect of conflict upon the nervous system was demonstrated dramatically by psychiatrist Jules Masserman several years ago in Chicago. He trained cats to press a lever in order to get pellets of food. The animals learned to operate the levers with no difficulty.

Then Dr. Masserman introduced the element of conflict. The cat was subjected to a sharp blast of compressed air just as it was ready to push the lever down. Inevitably the cat was in a bind, wanting to press the lever to get food, but fearful of the blast of air.

When the element of conflict was introduced, the emotional and physical condition of the cat deteriorated badly. All of the common signs of anxiety were present. The cat trembled, breathing rapidly in shallow breaths, with a rapid pulse. Its blood pressure increased, and the pupils dilated.

These evidences of tension and anxiety are identical with those experienced by a human being under severe stress and a conflict.

Dr. Masserman reported that when the laboratory cats were removed from the cages, they relaxed and showed none of the signs of anxiety evident during the tests. But when they were brought back to the cages, but not subjected to the blasts of air, the cats invariably showed all the original symptoms of an anxiety neurosis. The original environment triggered the anxiety response.

ANXIETY CAN LEAD TO CHANGE

Fortunately, there is a positive side to anxiety. It can provide motivation to change—to alter one's life situation and resolve conflicts. Guilt and conflict produce excessive anxiety, which is a most uncomfortable emotion. In seeking to be rid of the anxiety, one seeks relief of some sort.

Longing to retain our guilty secrets or maintain our destructive way of living, we go from doctor to doctor, hoping one of them will discover some physical malady and prescribe a pill to cure it.

When enough physicians have found no physical cause for the distress, the wise person then seeks a competent counselor to learn the real cause of the problem. We can thank God for anxiety, the divine warning system alerting us to the fact that there is an inner conflict demanding attention.

Very often it is not a single precipitating cause that produces the anxiety, but a combination of factors. The most serious anxiety neurosis I have encountered in recent years had not one but several unrelated sources.

Herb had an all-pervasive anxiety that virtually incapacitated him. He told me that he had had a normal childhood. In Primal Integration sessions, he relived with great

intensity being abandoned successively by his father and
mother, living with relatives, then being reunited years later
with his parents whom he scarcely knew.

A second source of his anxiety was an enormous load of
guilt. He had confessed it to God and felt that he was
forgiven. He had been forgiven by God but not by himself.
His primal confessions lasted two hours and involved not
simply repentance but deep, heart-felt remorse. He confessed from the depths of his being and only then did he feel
utterly forgiven by God and himself.

The third factor was that his diet was unbelievably
atrocious. When this was corrected, the last of his deep
anxiety disappeared. Since spirit, mind, and body work as a
unit and are inseparable, what affects one will influence the
other. Only when all three of those factors were resolved was
he permanently relieved of his paralyzing anxiety neurosis.

A young woman relived in a primal session the experience
of having attended a new school where she was ridiculed by
the other pupils. She ate her lunch alone and walked home
through side streets to avoid meeting any of the other
children. Each morning she was genuinely sick with fear
and apprehension, but her mother, with whom she could
not share the torture she was enduring, insisted that she get
up and go to school.

The young woman relived those horror-filled experiences with agonizing hysterical screams. She was relieved of
the encapsulated anxiety and tension that had plagued her
when she discharged the last of those repressed emotions of
fear and shame.

A LEGALISTIC RELIGION IS DESTRUCTIVE

Those who were reared in a judgmental, punitive home
environment or attended a legalistic church often grow up
with a conscience that is especially harsh.

A woman who had experienced a fundamentalist church background wrote me of the lasting damage it had done her:

> I was raised in churches where all our preachers could talk about was death, judgment day, hell, and the Second Coming. They also stressed the idea that many so-called Christians would discover on judgment day that they were not saved after all and would go to hell. There was much emphasis on questioning whether our conversion was genuine or not.

I have received many similar letters and have talked to a great many others who have reported the lasting damage done by that type of religious emphasis.

That was not the approach Jesus used. He received people with incredible tenderness, and we read that he came into the world "not to judge the world, but that the world might be saved through him" (John 3:17).

Children reared in a punitive home environment or who are exposed to religious legalism will carry some of those childhood emotions into adult life, at least in the unconscious mind.

It bears repetition: the emotions have no chronology. They are timeless. The event is in the past, but the emotion resides in adults in some form, as long as they live, or until they are able to relive the repressed emotions of fear, shame, guilt, anger, or inferiority and discharge them.

Meanwhile, remember that, as Mark Twain once said, "Heaven is ours by the grace of God. If it were by merit, you would stay out and your dog would go in." A theologian would put it differently, but in his trenchant way, Twain was uttering a profound truth. We do not win eternal life by our merits. We are so accustomed to winning promotions, pay raises, and other goodies as the result of hard work and exemplary conduct that it is difficult not to think of eternal life as something we earn.

The Bible makes it clear that we have eternal life as the result of what Christ has done for us; rewards in heaven will be given us as the result of what we have done for Christ. The thief on the cross had no time to clean up his act, only a momentary opportunity to confess his faith in Christ as the Son of God, and to him Jesus said, "Today, you will be with me in paradise" (Luke 23:43).

Though we fall a thousand times, God's limitless love and forgiveness reach out to us. All he asks is that we come to him in sincere repentance. He then restores us instantly to divine favor—for we are his children—and he loves us with an everlasting love. If, in our self-rejection we hesitate to believe the good news that Christ died for us, we miss the whole point of redemptive love. Christ on the cross enacted and demonstrated what has always been true about God: He loves us, forgives us, and welcomes us back from our wanderings.

BURIED GUILT

We have dealt with real guilt—wrongdoing accompanied by justifiable feelings of remorse—and false guilt, which creates the same emotions as genuine guilt, though the feelings are based on an erroneous concept of guilt. Now we must consider unconscious or repressed guilt. (I am talking about repressed *guilt*—not repressed anger.)

This can be the most damaging of all, for with buried guilt, people are not consciously aware of being wrong or of having violated any law of God or man. This often takes place when we rationalize our guilt. At a conscious level, we do not feel guilty; we simply bury our guilt, but the unconscious mind *never accepts a rationalization.*

When actual guilt is repressed, the inner judicial system goes into action and pronounces us guilty. Guilt must be either punished or forgiven. Since there is no repentance, thus no release, the inner judge exacts its penalty—punishment. Two things now take place. We may become accident-prone, illness-prone, or bad judgment-prone. We may make a bad business decision or become ill, for the inner judicial system is inexorable, implacable. It knows no plea bargaining, no "justice tempered with mercy."

Another manifestation of unconscious guilt is called projection. As guilty persons, unaware of what we are doing, we become critical. We blame others and become judgmental. It may take the form of moral judgment. Many flaming reformers are partially motivated by unconscious guilt. They keep it under the level of consciousness by condemnation of evil in others. This in no sense can be said of all moral crusaders, but it is obviously true in some instances.

UNIVERSAL GUILT

All are guilty, for all have sinned. It is the universal condition of humankind. Our only escape from divine or self-condemnation is to confess our wrongdoing, accept God's forgiveness, make restitution where appropriate, and then embark on a program of self-forgiveness, perhaps the most difficult of all to do.

This process involves affirming to the inner self the truth that since God has forgiven, accepted, and loves us, we must now forgive, accept, and love ourselves. This must be repeated often, for the average person has accused himself or herself mentally many times. Every remorseful feeling is an accusation. We can counteract damaging self-accusation by affirming the *truth:*

God forgives me, accepts me, and loves me. I now forgive and accept myself and will love myself properly.

CHAPTER SIX

Sex and Self-Esteem

I am not what I ought to be; I am not what I want to be, but by the grace of God I am not what I was, and I mean to be more like Christ.

Anonymous

Once there were certain things people couldn't talk about. Now they can't talk about anything else. And they are doing more than talk about it.

The pendulum has swung from neurotic sexual repression to exaggerated expression. In advertising, sex sells everything from soap to automobiles.

The aspect of human sexuality we are concerned with is guilt, which results in self-condemnation. This, in turn, is followed by a loss of self-esteem. And that is just another term for a feeling of inferiority.

ADULTERY

Because the sex drive is the strongest emotion God has given us, it can be the source of a vast amount of guilt. For instance, a national magazine conducted a survey of 100,000 women and discovered that whereas a study in 1975 showed that 40 percent of married women had been unfaithful to their husbands, in 1981 an astonishing 54 percent of married woman responding revealed that they had been unfaithful.

The report concluded that although there are many kinds of adultery, varying from one-night stands to long-term relationships, the typical person tends to go through a number of different phases.

In the first stage the women reportedly had felt *depressed*, often without any genuine sense of self-worth.

A second stage produced a type of *euphoria*. A woman's self-image is restored. She feels loved, appreciated, desirable. She tends at this point either to need no further reassurance, or the pleasurable sensation of being in love again is so great she decides to continue the relationship. If this is the decision, she begins to experience *guilt* feelings.

If she feels a sense of shame for having betrayed her husband, she may lose interest in her lover, and her husband becomes more desirable than before. The affirmation she has received has restored her self-confidence.

The next stage is *rationalization*. She finds ways to justify her behavior. Her husband does not appreciate her, or their incompatibility makes it impossible to sustain a warm relationship with him. She feels entitled to this new relationship.

Subsequently she may feel *gratitude* toward her husband for providing financial security, together with the euphoria of a new-found love. Or, in an effort to deny her guilt, she may accuse her husband of all manner of defects, thus promoting a domestic discord so severe that the only solution is to continue the relationship with her lover.

Ultimately she begins to feel a need for *resolution* of the situation. Whether she is aware of it consciously or not, at some level she senses that there must be some kind of closure. The fear that her husband will discover her duplicity, together with her inner conflict, produces a state of *confusion*. This in turn results in ambivilence. She becomes emotionally confused, wanting to hang onto the marriage, yet continue the affair. Her confusion continues until she finally reaches the final stage, either renouncing the marriage or giving up the lover. This may take ten months or many years, depending upon many factors.

Men appear to go through substantially the same stages of euphoria, guilt, rationalization, gratitude, confusion, and ultimate resolution.[1]

SEXUAL THOUGHTS

In addition to the guilt induced by marital unfaithfulness, there are other aspects to sexual guilt. Many people, reared in a legalistic religious environment, feel guilty over their sexual thoughts. They interpret these as lust and are convinced that they have committed adultery. Unfortunately, false guilt is just as destructive as real guilt and results in the same self-hate, with consequent loss of self-worth.

The sex drive, if it has no suitable expression, causes many people to indulge in sexual fantasies. The more they try to put such ideas out of their minds, the more tenaciously the thoughts cling. Some, beset with such a preoccupation, feel very guilty and imagine they have committed a terrible sin.

A woman once came to me with what she termed a serious problem. She said, "I have this terrible confusion about the Trinity. Can you explain it to me?" I had seldom known anyone to become so preoccupied and tense about a theological problem and suspected she had some other difficulty which she was reluctant to disclose. However, I spent a few minutes explaining that the doctrine of the

Trinity was very complex and that we could not be very dogmatic about any one concept, since it was a deep mystery.

"But," I said, "I imagine that in addition to this difficulty, you may have something else on your mind that is troubling you. Would you care to tell me what it is? Perhaps we can get to the root of an even more perplexing problem." She looked startled and was silent for a few moments.

Then, "Well, I guess there is something else. I've been having this conflict about, well, about sex. I hesitated to bring it up, but perhaps I might as well." And she began, rather hesitantly, to share some of her feelings of guilt about her preoccupation with sexual thoughts and feelings.

I was able to reassure her by telling her that the emotions she was experiencing were perfectly normal. The difficulty she had in putting these thoughts out of her mind was based on the fact that she felt guilty entertaining such feelings, and the more she tried to suppress them, the more they clung. I said, "Let's suppose that the number seven is evil. Now, I want you to put the number seven out of your mind entirely. Don't dwell on seven, because it is evil, wrong. Seven must never enter your mind. Now what are you thinking about?"

"Seven," she said, laughing.

"It is impossible to expel a thought from your mind by saying, 'I won't think about it.' The unconscious mind doesn't hear the negative *won't*, and you are stuck with an obsessive thought."

I added, "Acceptance is the first step. Accept the thought as neither good nor bad—just a thought. Do not resist the thought or emotion, or your preoccupation with the battle will intensify. Gently take the thought and hang it on a hook over in the corner of your mind. When and if it floats back, there is no need to feel guilty. Just push it over to the left side of your mind again, much as you would put a cat out of the house if it kept creeping back through a hole in the screen door. Even the saints and mystics report that they have been troubled by these burlesque thoughts and images. It's a part of our humanity. Once the unwanted thought is gently pushed to one side, substitute a positive thought. The words of a lovely hymn are appropriate:" And then I recited:

> When evil thought molest,
> With this I shield my breast,
> May Jesus Christ be praised.

CHILDREN WHO ARE MOLESTED

There are other aspects of sexual guilt. For instance, approximately 35 percent of women who come to the Burlingame Counseling Center have been sexually molested as children. (Some of the twenty-five other counseling centers affiliated with us report a much higher figure.) Many of the women were totally unaware of this until in primal sessions the unconscious mind gave up its painful secret.

There is more of this going on in good, substantial homes than we ever dreamed of, according to psychiatrist Robert Wallerstein, professor of psychiatry at the University of California at San Francisco. Sociologist Joyce Spencer says that frequently, the incestuous father can't sustain a relationship with a mature woman, so he turns to a child. While a young girl may sense that something is wrong, she is obeying her father—and her mother often is condoning the arrangement or at least prefers not to know. In the end, the victims may blame themselves.

Most children choose to remain silent for fear they will not be believed, and sometimes because of threats. Children then live in fear of discovery and of punishment if they tell anyone about their secret. This creates an enormous amount of guilt, insecurity, and consequent feelings of worthlessness.

A San Jose, California, group called Parents United has dealt with 3,500 families in which incest took place. Authorities say that this is only the tip of the iceberg in one community.

Our experience in dealing with sexual molestation reveals that the most frequent culprits are uncles, followed by grandfathers, then stepfathers, fathers, and finally brothers. At the bottom of the list in terms of frequency is the neighbor, usually a lonely man who is kind to children. The stranger (the one mothers warn their children about) who lures the little girl into his car is the least frequent perpetrator of this crime.

Incestuous relationships occur most frequently between a relative and little girls, but molestation of small boys often occurs. In either case, the children feel a sense of shame. A minister related, "My high school principal was after me during an entire school year. He didn't succeed, but he was very persistent. I never told my parents for some obscure reason, perhaps because he was a friend of the family and I thought I might not be believed. Besides, I never shared anything of importance with my parents. They had never mentioned the subject of sex, and I must have felt that this was something they couldn't handle. Later, some boy with more courage than I had blew the whistle on him, and he left town in the middle of the night. His car stalled on the railroad track, as I learned later, and he barely escaped with his life as a freight train smashed into his car. He was left with nothing but the clothes on his back, unemployed, and only a scandalized community to turn to for help. I felt quite pleased when I first learned of it, though now I can feel some compassion for the poor misguided man."

THE "SOLITARY VICE"

Psychiatrist Tom Leland quotes from a book with the remarkable title, *Safe Counsel: A Complete Sexual Science and a Guard to Purity and Physical Manhood, Advice to Maiden, Wife, and Mother on Love, Courtship, and Marriage*. Published in 1895, this book contains the following gem:

> Chastity is the purest and brightest jewel in human character. . . . The most valuable and useful organs of the body are those which are capable of the greatest dishonor, abuse, and corruption. The organ concerning the uses of which I am to speak has been and continues to be made one of the chief instruments of man's immorality, shame, disease, and death. . . . I first deal with the destructive sin of self-abuse. There can be little doubt that vast numbers of boys are guilty of this practice. In many cases the degrading habit has been taught by others, that is, by older boys at school, where association largely results in mutual corruption. With others, the means of sensual gratification is found out by personal action. . . .
>
> Thousands of youths and young men have only to look in the looking glass to see the portrait of one guilty of this loathsome sin. The effects are plainly discernable in the boy's appearance. The face and hands become pale and bloodless. The eye is destitute of its natural fire and luster. The flesh is soft and flabby, the muscles limp and lacking a healthy firmness. In cases where the habit has become confirmed and where the system has been drained of this vital force, it is seen in positive ugliness, in a pale and cadaverous appearance, slovenly gait, slouchy walk, and an impaired memory.[2]

I would suggest that the author of that gem had a problem and was projecting his own conflict and guilt onto a society already loaded with false guilt concerning human sexuality.

Today psychiatrists, ministers, and psychologists are of the opinion that masturbation is, as one prominent minister-writer put it, "God's gift to the young and the unmarried."[3]

I once listened to a deeply troubled young woman diagnosed as a paranoid schizophrenic, who had been locked up in a mental hospital four times. She had shared with me the cause of her "mental illness." I said, "God isn't interested in the slightest about masturbation—not any more than if you were bitten by a mosquito and scratched the place where it bit you."

She looked astounded and at first unbelieving, then said with a trace of anger in her voice, "Why didn't they tell me that in the mental hospital?"

I replied, "I suppose you didn't trust them enough to tell them your problem, or they didn't take the time to try to find out what your real difficulty was." She wrote me later to report that everything was taking on new meaning.

"Life is beautiful," she wrote.

Yes, false guilt over sex not only can produce self-hate just as real guilt can; it also has sent countless numbers of people to mental institutions, feeling they have offended God in some way.

We Are Sexual-Physical-Spiritual Beings

But sex concerns much more than the genital aspect of one's physical nature. It has to do with the totality of one's personality. It relates to the way we feel and think, and half a hundred subtle distinctions. The ridiculous drive for a kind of unisex in which all sexual differences are wiped out is one result of an otherwise commendable drive for women's rights. As with many revolutionary movements, the proponents have ridden beyond their destination and spawned a great number of absurdities.

Let's look at the Oedipal complex, one of the valuable concepts which Freud has given us. In brief, this is the instinctual drive of a little boy to win his mother. Around the age of four or five, he develops an intensive and possessive love for her. In his childish mind, he fantasizes growing up and marrying her. But this involves a conflict. What about Daddy? He may have fantasies of his father getting lost and never returning, or of dying of old age. At any rate, he disposes of his father, the third part of the triangle. Now in his own mind, he possesses mother. In one sense, it is a kind of rehearsal for life; at a deeper level, it is his way of having his masculinity validated by mother.

If she accepts and affirms this little man who has become her suitor, she becomes his first conquest. He is acting out the role of a man—a little man to be sure, but still a man. If, during this stage, he feels rejected by his mother, this is a severe hindrance to his fantasy of marrying her. He then receives no validation of his masculinity. Nature's apparent goal in this interesting drama has been thwarted.

The same thing happens with the little girl, in relation to her father. If Daddy takes time to hold her and cuddle her, and she feels that she has "won" him in fantasy, her femininity is affirmed. She is now a "woman." She has a secret in her seductive little heart, and the nearest she may ever come to revealing it is to confide, "I love you, Daddy, and I want to marry you when I grow up."

The small child almost invariably represses the memory of this experience, partly out of guilt over having dispossessed the parent of the same sex.

The little girl whose father rejects her, or never has time to cuddle and play with her, may thereafter in adult life be reticent or even hostile in relationships with men, sexually frigid, or may lack a sense of feminine identity. The same thing holds true for the little boy who feels rejected, in that

he tends to lack a sense of his own masculine identity. A
vague sense of inferiority is generated. The adult may know,
intellectually, that he or she is quite adequate, yet lack a
proper sense of sexual identity.

A HOMOSEXUAL IS CHANGED

Norman, age thirty-six, came to the Burlingame
Counseling Center because he was troubled by his bi-
sexuality. Although he had frequent homosexual encounters, he always felt terribly guilty afterward and resolved not
to become involved again, but before long, he would find
himself seeking a sexual relationship with a man.

His primal sessions were alternately with a male and a
female therapist. Though his primals at first dealt with the
early years of childhood and infancy, including a birth
experience, only at the conclusion of his sessions did he
encounter the problem of his homosexuality.

The session began with positive feelings. Music was
played on the stereo system. He began to thank Christ for
his love.

As Gounod's *Sanctus* was playing, Norman experienced
religious ecstasy for some minutes. He writes of the rest of
his session:

> I began to breathe very deeply, as instructed. I started to
> feel pain in my stomach. I had learned this meant fear. Dr.
> Osborne asked me what I was afraid of. I said, "My
> homosexuality." I began to call on Jesus to help me. Then I
> tried to force the acute pain out of my stomach up through
> my chest and out my throat.
>
> I started to call, "Help me, help me, help me!" I began to
> kick and flail my arms and screamed, "Turn loose, turn
> loose. Get out, get out, get out of me." This went on for a
> long time.

For half an hour Norman was all over the mat, pounding, screaming, choking, pleading for help to get "it" out. (It is interesting to note that in such an experience subjects can stop any time they choose. They are not unconscious or out of control.)

> I could feel the "thing" moving up from my stomach toward my throat. I rolled over on my side, gagging, trying to force the pain and fear out. Lying on my side with my back in a reverse arch, my feet almost touching my back bone, my mouth wide open to the point of hurting, I made a series of long, deep groans. The pain was leaving and going out my mouth, and finally it was gone.
>
> I was exhausted. I definitely felt something had changed within me. Then Dr. Osborne and I embraced. I was crying and praising Jesus for several minutes. The new feeling was so wonderful! Dr. Osborne told me he had been in deep prayer for me. There were people at home praying for me, too. We both praised God!

As I observed Norman in the session just described, I had the eerie feeling that I was witnessing an exorcism. Whatever "it" was, it came out with great difficulty and pain. He could feel it moving slowly upward from deep within him.

> In my next session with Josephine [the therapist], after the initial deep breathing, I felt empty inside. But my stomach didn't hurt anymore. The pain was all gone. She wanted to know what I felt. She had me do some more deep breathing and asked what I was feeling. I told her, "Love." She asked where the love came from, and I told her, "Everywhere, from God. He gives us love."
>
> Josephine then had me breathe in God's love deeply, and let it flow through my body, starting with my head and going, joint by joint, to my toes. I repeated this several times. It was the most pleasant and peaceful experience of my life!

She asked me later what I felt, and I told her I felt the pain and conflict were all gone, and now my whole body was filled with love. It felt good all over!

I felt a *whole* man, with a complete body for the first time in my life. I have no desire for homosexual relations. The feeling is gone.

Later, in Dr. Osborne's office, I picked up a book depicting various anatomical aspects of both the male and female bodies. Before, when I had seen such explicit details of a male body, it had excited me. Now I had a total lack of sexual interest. I had always had a sexual response to both males and females. Now it is solely an interest in females. I'm whole, normal! Thank God.

After returning home, Norman wrote, "I told my friend I had no further need for homosexual relationships. My relationship with my wife has greatly improved, for I can give 100 percent of myself. Wonderful. And I have a whole new attitude toward life. I'm *one!*"

"I'M A NEUTER"

A woman who, in an initial counseling session in my office, could not raise her eyes from the floor, relived in her primal sessions the incessant beatings she had endured at the hands of her sadistic mother. She had married a man who was as sadistic emotionally as her mother had been physically. With almost no self-esteem, she felt inferior, guilty, and worthless, despite a good mind. She wrote later:

In my primal sessions, I felt emptiness over having been a neuter all these years, not being either female or male, just a nothing. I wept uncontrollably. In all the years I've been married, I have not been able to feel feminine, and my husband cannot arouse feminine feelings in me. In fact, I feel nothing.

I know from that last primal session that the problem is deeper than I thought. It is deeper than rejection by my mother and the hatred I felt for her. It is my lack of ever having been able to feel like a female. That is the deep underlying problem I need to resolve.

Subsequently, she made enormous progress in accepting her innate femininity. In time she found the strength to stand up to her husband. She went back to school and took courses that prepared her to accept a teaching position. She gained a sense of strength and identity she had never known in more than forty years. Psychiatrist Paul L. Warner writes:

> God loves us the way he created us. This means that there is never any reason for us to feel guilty or ashamed of the way our bodies look, the feelings that take place within our bodies, and the temptation thoughts that come as a result of any feelings which we experience. . . . All of these things help us identify with Jesus Christ in his humanity, rather than give us any reason to feel ashamed or guilty. . . . It is necessary for us to experience guilt only when we wilfully decide to break the moral law of God. . . . Only giving in to the temptation can be wrong. This "giving in" may be nothing more than mental assent, and that is where our sin begins.[4]

Psychologist William James of Harvard once said that the first essential step in resolving a problem is to accept it. By this he did not mean approval of a situation, but acceptance of it *as it is*. We cannot resolve a difficulty until we are willing to face it.

The pronouncement of William James is an echo of the psalmist's statement, "Behold, thou desirest truth in the inward being" (Psalm 51:6). This is affirmed by Jesus when he declared that "You will know the truth, and the truth will make you free" (John 8:32).

CHAPTER SEVEN

Self-Esteem and Our Parents

The pleasure we derive from doing favors is partly the feeling it gives us that we are not altogether worthless.

Eric Hoffer

I observed a young woman for over an hour as she went about her duties, working with numerous people. I felt that I had never seen such an outgoing, spontaneous unselfconscious person. She appeared to have no self-doubts, as she flashed a warm smile at everyone, old and young. She was a tireless, efficient, altogether charming young woman.

Finally, I approached her and said, "I want to talk to you." I said it rather brusquely, wondering if she would feel apprehensive.

She just smiled and said, "Yes?"

I said, "I've been watching you for over an hour. I want to hazard a guess about you and your parents."

She smiled and said, "Oh?"

"I have a feeling your parents loved each other very much, that they seldom if ever fought, and that you received unconditional love from them."

"Yes," she said, "of course! Why?" as if this were quite commonplace.

"I want also to speculate that your parents were well-integrated people, with no morbid feelings of guilt or inferiority."

She looked a bit surprised and said, "Sure, why?"

I realized I was dealing with a beautifully integrated young woman who had never suspected how much trauma an average child endures in the growing up process.

Finally, I said, "You're such a caring, spontaneous, unselfconscious person, I find you quite unique."

She again looked surprised, then said, "Why, yes, I suppose so; it's the only way to be."

I congratulated her on having such emotionally mature parents, and for the way she manifested her own wholeness.

If you had had two parents who were able consistently to give unconditional love, who were emotionally mature in every way and used exquisite wisdom in the rearing of children, you would probably have lots of self-esteem. Unfortunately, your parents had parents, who had parents, who were—like most humans—lacking in some respects.

Without blaming our parents in the slightest, since they did their best, suppose we have a look at some of the problems they and we encountered during our childhoods.

Discovering the Truth About the Past

A young married woman came to our counseling center for help with her marriage. I sensed from her voice and manner that there had been some form of deprivation in her childhood that could be affecting the marriage. She assured me she had had a happy childhood.

However, in her primal sessions, when she was regressed back to early childhood, she wept hour after hour. She discovered something she had never known consciously: Her childhood had been very unhappy. She had not received adequate love, and there were countless traumas, major and minor, which she had pushed out of her consciousness.

Martha had been told by her mother and father so often how greatly she was loved that she had never doubted it. What she couldn't understand was why, at age forty-two, she always felt like a six-year-old child when visiting her parents, and had migraine headaches for a week or so after returning home. And she had difficulty finding the source of her lengthy depression after her parents' annual visit. She loved her parents, she insisted, and they loved her. She had had a wonderful childhood. Her mother had regaled her with so many stories about the happy childhood that Martha couldn't tell which incidents were memories and which were events told by her mother.

She found out in her Primal Integration sessions. In the primal room, deep into her childhood, as though on a split screen, she experienced being three years old, while with the adult part of her mind she was hearing the therapist and integrating it all into one relevant whole. She was there at age three and being brutally whipped by her mother for some innocent indiscretion. She relived being sent to her room without supper, crying herself to sleep, her mother coldly demanding the next morning that she straighten up and act like a nice little girl. A score or more of other beatings were reexperienced with acute intensity. Her screams and pleadings did not soften her mother's implacable firmness. Hour after hour she explored her tortured past with a cold, punitive mother and an aloof father.

Sitting up during one session, she said, "I would never have believed all that happened to me if somone had told me. I had completely blocked it out. I now know why. It was too painful. During those beatings I was sure they hated me.

I *had* to bury it, because it was too painful to retain in my conscious memory. But I need to go back and relive it all. I'm getting relief by expressing the hurt and anger I had to repress in order to survive. Let's go," and she lay down and was breathed down again into her childhood.

The amazing thing one experiences during primal sessions is that it feels better to relive that repressed pain than it does to experience the deadness resulting from holding it down in the unconscious. "I am more alive," one man said. "I can feel my body; it's part of me, for the first time. And I now know I have been somewhat depressed all my life, and I never knew it. I had no basis for judgment, for I have never been otherwise. My wife and my friends tell me that they can see the difference, and I can feel it. I'm coming alive for the first time in thirty-eight years."

A woman told me that she knew her childhood had been rotten, and she often wept bitterly about it. But she said, "I don't get any lasting relief from crying. Why is that?"

"We call that 'leaking,' " I said. "Primal Pain produces weeping of a different kind. One can derive a mild relief from crying about current hurts or childhood deprivation; but in a primal experience, the individual is *reliving*, not just remembering, the event. There is a vast difference between having a good cry, and reexperiencing the primal pain while reliving the event. Those who have had Primal Integration know the difference at once."

At least 98 percent of all that transpired before the age of five has been forgotten—that is, buried in the unconscious. But it is accessible in primal sessions and when relived, can rid the personality of neurotic symptoms.

Sigmund Freud points out, "The experience of the first five years of childhood exerts decisive influence on our lives, one which later events oppose in vain. . . . What a child has experienced and not understood by the age of two he may never again remember, except in his dreams . . . At any time in later years, however, they may break into his life with obsessive compulsiveness, direct his actions, force him to like or dislike people, and often decide the choice of his love-object by the preference which often cannot be rationally defended."[1]

THE LACK OF ATTENTION AND TIME

Children are not born with self-esteem; they derive it from having their parents take time to nurture them; by being held and touched, talked to and listened to. The child needs to have his feelings validated.

A child never experiences any greater fear than that of being abandoned or unloved by his parents. He desperately fears being ignored or rejected. In fact, a child derives his only sense of identity from being loved, cared for, noticed, and approved. Without such affirmation, a child grows up with little sense of being worthwhile, thus with no sense of identity.

We never outgrow this need. The degrees we award, honors we bestow, and the titles we give and receive are all adult counterparts of the love the child needed. We seek it, hunger for it, and are often warped if denied it. We are "tin cuppers," waiting for someone to fill our cups. Love can come in the form of approval, of being noticed, of being listened to, and of being complimented. At a deeper level, we need affirmation as well as approval and acceptance. If denied love, we suffer at some deep level.

Some psychologists believe adult anxiety can be related to the fear of disapproval, that originally we feared that our mother would not love us if we did something of which she disapproved. For the anxious person, the love and approval of almost everyone he meets is required for him to feel some measure of safety. In quest of approval and love, the anxious person does many things to placate those near him, often with considerable resentment and hostility he dare not express. When he does something for himself, he will feel selfish or ungiving.[2]

More than twenty-five years ago, a study described the "marasmus," or physical wasting away of infants who suddenly lost their mothers. Such infants would refuse to eat, and eventually died, even when force-fed. In one study, for example, ninety-one infants raised in foundling homes in the United States and Canada were followed. All these infants were physically very well cared for. In spite of this care, it was reported that most of the infants appeared to be very depressed, and many also seemed quite anxious. They did not grow as rapidly as other infants; they did not gain weight, and some even lost weight. Of the ninety-one infants studied, thirty-four died in spite of good food and meticulous medical care. Among those who survived, almost all showed various degrees of physical and emotional retardation. But it isn't only in orphanages and foundling homes that this happens. It occurs in varying degrees and sundry ways in the best of homes.

THE NEED FOR AFFIRMATION

One of the commonest mistakes parents make is to reject the child's feelings. Jimmy comes into the kitchen fifteen minutes before dinner. "I'm hungry," he says.

"No, you're not hungry. It isn't dinner time yet," he is told. The basic message is, your feelings don't count. They're not valid. He should get a reply such as, "Yes, I'm hungry, too, and we're going to eat in just a few minutes. It's hard to wait when we're hungry, isn't it?"

Susie has an accident and cries about her cut finger. "It hurts!" she wails. The anguish seems out of all proportion to the tiny cut, so mother tells her, "Oh, don't be such a baby. It doesn't hurt all that much. Go to the bathroom and bandage it."

Mother's response tells Susie feelings don't matter, and mother doesn't care if she hurts. Of course, an opposite extreme, equally damaging, is to make an enormous fuss over a small hurt and thus teach the child that all minor pains warrant a gigantic emotional upheaval. Neither extreme is called for.

Parents often ask, "How should I treat my child?" The answer is, "How do you treat someone you love a great deal?" Obviously with concern and loving care. You validate their feelings; you listen to them; you do not deprecate them or their emotions; you pay attention to them.

One woman said, "My mother was a pretty good cook and a fairly good housekeeper, but she was a magnificent mother. She'd throw the dishes in the sink and say, 'Hey, kids, let's go for an adventure in the woods.' And we'd go hiking, or we would walk to the lake and go out in a rowboat. We learned we were more important to her than inanimate things like dishes and kitchen floors. And we had a ball! She was fun to be with. She didn't have to tell us she loved us. We *felt* loved, because she put us first in her life."

Swiss Psychoanalyst Alice Miller writes, "Sometimes I ask myself whether it will ever be possible for us to grasp the extent of the loneliness and desertion to which we were exposed as children." She does not mean children who were physically neglected by their parents, but normal, gifted children who became the victims of their parents' inability to love properly.

She adds: "In order to develop a healthy sense of identity and self-worth, the child needs to be taken seriously and respected as a person by his mother. He 'makes use of her' as a mirror, the baby gazing at his mother, while the mother gazes back, the infant absorbing love and caring in the interchange of emotions."[3] Thus, Miller maintains, is self-worth achieved by the child.

At a weekend retreat for a group of men in Texas, I mentioned the fact that a typical parent will give a child twenty criticisms or putdowns to one bit of praise. I added that the ratio needed to be reversed; that is, twenty compliments and affirmations for every negative comment.

I noticed a group of men in a huddle after the session. The next morning, I discovered what they had been talking about. One of the men announced they planned to start a Twenty to One Club, with the goal of giving their children twenty positive comments to every critical putdown. They were enthusiastic about it and agreed they would check up on each other from time to time. I complimented them. They were moving in the right direction.

Some parents have noticed that a child will have an almost unending series of colds or upper respiratory tract ailments—asthma and sinus problems as well as colds. When told that the child is manifesting a need for love, a typical parent replies that no child was ever loved more. How the parents feel about this is meaningless. Nothing matters but what the *child* feels. Many a loved child feels rejection, inferiority, shame, and guilt—just plain miserable—and has no way of communicating this to his parents. Frequent respiratory tract ailments are the tears turned inward.

The child has an almost insatiable need for affirmation. Being told he is loved may not register, particularly if he is being admonished to try harder, do better, be more polite, be kinder, study, be cleaner, and be nice. The unattainable goal is too great a burden, and the child cannot hear the words "I love you" because of all the criticisms received.

THE POWER OF TOUCH

The people who come to the Burlingame Counseling Center are a cross section of society—including ministers, truck drivers, housewives, psychologists, psychiatrists, scientists, office workers, missionaries, and many other categories. The vast majority report that they received inadequate holding and touching early in life. Children receive a large part of their sense of security and affirmation from being held and cuddled.

The power of touch even among adults was dramatically illustrated by a psychological experiment. A young woman went repeatedly to a pay phone in the lobby of a busy office building, each time leaving a coin in the return coin slot. After another person had used the phone, she would ask, "Did you find the coin I left in the coinbox?" Some she touched lightly on the arm as she asked. Others she did not touch. Those touched returned the coin. A majority of the others did not.

A few people, due to childhood deprivation, resent any physical contact, but a majority of adults respond positively to an appropriate touch. Very few of us received enough in infancy and childhood. Those who did usually welcome it in adult life. Most of those who did not receive it are still hungry for touch; some who got little or none in childhood have said to themselves, "I don't need it" (a lie): "I don't want it. Don't touch me!" The lie is a self-protective defense.

THE RESULTS OF POOR PARENTING

Robert Lea writes of the painful experience when his wife committed suicide. A policeman rang the bell at their home and told Lea his wife had leaped to her death from the

Golden Gate bridge. Desolated and heartbroken, he went to his wife's room and found her final note, tucked into a book she had been reading:

> "Dearest, what can I say? . . . I can't take the pain of living any longer. My love, *you're not to blame.* The children are not to blame . . . I'm sorry it's Easter, but I can't wait. . . . —Deb."
>
> The note had been stuck near the front of the book, where a paragraph was circled in black ink, the last two words underlined: "Feelings of self-hate are part of an ongoing process that includes sabotaging decisions, moves and activities against one's self, and *ultimately suicide.*"[4]

Deborah had had two years of psychoanalysis in her twenties and more therapy in her forties to no avail.

Since all excessiveness, such as self-hate and deep depression, has roots that reach back to childhood, it is safe to say that Deborah did not derive a sense of self-worth in childhood; for it is in childhood that the foundation is laid for our self-esteem or self-hate.

The child who is overcoerced, pushed beyond his or her capacity, and not given sufficient love and approval, grows up with self-hate. This may be manifested in masochism —the unconscious will to fail—or it can take the form of depression, physical symptoms, or, in extreme cases, suicide.

Freud maintained, "The child feels itself inferior when it perceives it is not loved and so does the adult as well. . . . The sense of inferiority and the sense of guilt are exceedingly difficult to distinguish."[5] Our staff has validated this by listening for thousands of hours to people in Primal Integration sessions. Primal patients regressed to infancy and early childhood relive in infinite detail the traumas of those years.

Most parents, even if they do not spank, threaten and execute a series of explicit punishments. But they do not stop there, for they cannot accept the possibility that their children obey only through fear of consequences, their wills left intact for various forms of inner rebellion, disloyalty, and revenge. Parents marshal the age-old devices; they shame, they ignore, they snipe at deviation with a thousand psychic devices. They will never admit their intent to themselves—to kill the judgment and the will of the child where it deviates from their own. But to some extent every parent subconsciously seeks his own immortality, wants the child to be a carbon copy of himself, neurotic or healthy, and he signals this intention to the child in a thousand ways. . . .

Parents are to be all-giving, strong, wise, patient, virtuous, powerful, incorruptible, rich, immortal, coura- geous, and healthy. They must be impervious to the frustrations of life, the limitations of reality, and the gradual erosion of time. Whenever parents fail in this, they are despised. Did mother fall down and break a leg? How could she be so foolish as not to see the stick she tripped on; so unbalanced as to fall; so despicably weak that her bones would crack? Was father an alcoholic? How could he retreat so far from his role as immortal conqueror, master of both the world and his own reactions to it? Patients rage at every folly, failure, defeat, and limitation, every place where parents showed the slightest vulnerability.[6]

THE SCHOOL AND SELF-ESTEEM

But it is not only misguided parenting that causes neurosis. Primal hurts often are inflicted by unfeeling teachers, relatives, and by peers.

A fifty-nine-year-old woman, writing to "Dear Abbey," said that when she was sixteen, she had not been invited to a party because she wore a heavy brace on her leg. The hostess had told her that she would not enjoy the party, since she could not dance.[7]

After forty-three years, she could still feel the hurt, indicative of the fact that emotions have no chronology.

Sometimes thoughtless or heartless teachers do untold damage to a child's sensitive emotional structure. I recall the pain that showed in the face of a forty-five-year-old man as he told me how a teacher had humiliated him in front of the entire class, using him as an example of how not to dress and act.

There are genetic differences in children, to be sure. Some are very sensitive, while others are more able to ignore insults. But often the children who seem unaffected by criticism or humiliation have simply repressed the shame and hurt. Burying it does not get rid of it. It simply goes into dead storage in the unconscious, there to produce its deplorable litter of emotional or physical distortions. The more aggressive child may survive criticism and ridicule. He may become sadistic and take out his hurt on smaller children without ever sensing that he is simply displacing his anger onto defenseless children.

Or he may become destructive. Consider the multi-billion dollar loss from school vandalism throughout the United States. Imagine how much rage those young vandals are expressing at their teachers, at the entire educational system, and at life. School should not be a place where children are humiliated and suffer ignominious failure, but where, at their own speed and within their own limits, they can succeed in learning. Children instinctively want to learn, hence their ten thousand questions. But when the educational material is beyond them or presented in a manner that turns them off, they understandably become hostile and vengeful. One might well say that the vandals are sending the school system and parents a powerful message. Many turned-off children are lost to society, and the innocent taxpayer pays the bill for the vandalized school property.

A woman told me that in the third grade she was forced to stand up before the class while the teacher ridiculed her for being dirty and having matted hair.

"I came from a rotten home," she said. "My mother was a slob. She took no pains with us. So we grew up like little animals."

After that terrible experience, little Emily set fire to the school and burned it to the ground.

I said, "Though I don't officially condone arson, I assure you that I understand."

PARENTS ARE THE KEY TO SELF-ESTEEM

Small children feel anxiety over mother's disapproval long before they are able to give a rational explanation of their feelings. The mother-child relationship is all-important to infants, who are utterly dependent upon her for their survival. They rely upon her not only for the fulfilling of their physical needs, but for their security as well. They respond positively to her smile, and with tension and anxiety to her frown. For the very young infant, mother is the major source of satisfaction and emotional security, and for the development of self-esteem.

Alfred Adler believed that all neurosis and failure of the child to develop normal self-esteem were expressions of inferiority and disappointment. He writes, "Every bodily or mental attitude clearly indicates its origin in a striving for power and carries within itself the ideal of . . . perfection and infallibility. When this drive is frustrated, he will seek some form of gratification, even if it is only a fantasy. In order to overcome his feeling of inferiority, he will try to dominate and control his environment. This may be his family, an organization he is involved in, some movement, club, or society. If he cannot dominate it, he will withdraw from it and either establish a competing one or predict the downfall of the rejected group. He will then be vindicated."[8]

Adler pointed out that many of the outstanding men of history have had some physical handicap which, in less aggressive individuals, might have caused them to withdraw. He called this "organ inferiority," which includes such things as physical deformity, speech defects, being diminutive in size, or ill health. There come to mind such people as Napoleon, Franklin D. Roosevelt, Kaiser Wilhelm, and Adler himself, who suffered from poor health. Such people compensate for their inferiority with a "will to power." This is a means of delivering people from their sense of inferiority or weakness and contributes to their sense of dominating their environment. Thus they are no longer powerless, weak, or inferior.

I recall a woman whom I came to know quite well, who had been born with only one arm. She told me that her mother had gently but firmly told her, early in life, that she need not feel inferior to anyone else. "My mother insisted that I could learn to do anything anyone else could. She gave me no special privileges. I had to do my share of housework as I grew up. I learned not to expect special consideration. I was not permitted any self-pity, and I've never had any. I know I'm not normal physically, but I don't *feel* inadequate in any sense. I have lived a perfectly normal life."

But there are children who are handicapped by being derided for their real or imagined defects. "Your grades show you're not going to be as smart as your brother, so you'd sure better develop your personality if you want to amount to anything." "You're sure not going to win any beauty prizes, so you'd better develop your mind if you want to succeed." "With your kind of personality, who'd ever want to hire you?" There are a hundred variations on the

SELF-ESTEEM AND OUR PARENTS

theme of "You're not good enough." Thus inferiority feelings are developed by the very people to whom children look for approval.

Aggressive people seek to compensate for inadequacy feelings, and if all goes well, they may achieve significantly. If they are frustrated in their drives for power, they may become aggressively hostile. This can range from sarcasm to being physically sadistic. If thwarted in a creative solution, they may become criminals. If their aggression is buried, they may become masochistic and unconsciously punish themselves through sickness or by failing. All of this takes place at an unconscious level, of course. Since 85 to 90 percent of all our decisions and choices are motivated by unconscious drives, we are unaware of our neurotic motivation.

NEUROTIC COMPENSATION FOR INADEQUACY

As Adler pointed out, one compensates for feelings of inferiority or inadequacy, but there are creative and destructive compensations. A man who is driven neuroti- cally to compensate for childhood pain is not free. He must always make one more big deal, establish one more branch, make one more million, establish one more new depart- ment, or make one more conquest. The neurotic drive for power is a dead-end street.

Other ways of dealing with anxiety derived from primal pain are alcohol and drugs, which deaden some of the brain centers temporarily and allay the anxiety.

Compulsions often take the place of pills. We can become terribly busy. We feel better when we have an endless list of phone calls to answer or important people to see. Attention seeking, record smashing, and name dropping are other forms of compensation—all neurotic—for they do not provide ultimate satisfaction.

These various reaction patterns can be categorized under four general headings, defined by psychiatrist Karen Horney:

1. Neurotic striving for power, a struggle for domination and prestige whereby the individual seeks to become so powerful that no one can hurt him.

2. Neurotic striving for affection, inordinate and indiscriminate expression of an otherwise normal drive.

3. Neurotic submissiveness, in which the individual subordinates all his needs to those of others in the hope that by so submitting he will be protected from harm; and

4. Neurotic withdrawal, a retreat from all contact with other persons in an attempt to avoid even the risk of danger (rejection). . . . In his attempt to resolve the conflict situation and so achieve a feeling of unity, the neurotic person creates a deceptive *idealized* image which he believes to be himself, or someone he ought to be or could be.

It is seldom a single traumatic act which produces a neurotic personality, although this does happen. Far more often it is the daily reaction of the child to parents who are in some degree incapable of giving consistent mature love.[9]

A highly creative and productive professional man said,

I know that my parents loved me. They demonstrated it in a thousand ways, but *something was missing.* Something they did or didn't do left me with a terrible drive to be busy. My busyness has been a good thing in one way. I have produced. In another way, it has been terribly destructive. If I am not busy, I am restless, full of anxiety. I must be doing something every minute. I enjoy working and feel anxious when I'm not. If I'm not busy, I must read or make lists of things to do. A vague, gnawing restlessness drives me. I'm not driving; I'm *driven*. I think I picked up my father's inferiority complex by osmosis, and on top of that, I was consistently accused of being lazy. To win parental approval, I had to be busy, get things done. By an act of the will, I can sit down and rest, and I can take vacations, but it is not a naturally spontaneous thing. The voices in my head are still urging me to get busy, don't rest, the devil has work for idle hands. I can mute the voices, but never completely silence them, for they have penetrated my nervous system. Every nerve fiber is urging me on—pushing and driving. I have to be busy to survive, but at the cost of inner serenity.

Thus are neuroses created by loving, caring parents. In another chapter, we will see what steps people can take to rid themselves of their neurotic hangups.

CHAPTER EIGHT

Self-Esteem and Depression

Faith means believing what is incredible, or it is no virtue at all. Hope means hoping when things are hopeless, or it is no virtue at all; and charity means pardoning what is unpardonable, or it is no virtue at all.

G. K. Chesterton

There are different kinds of depression and numerous causes. It can affect men and women differently. A recent book by science writer Maggie Scarf, *Unfinished Business: Pressure Points in the Lives of Women*, points out that two to six times as many women as men suffer from deep depression. The author studied many case histories, observed women under treatment in psychiatric clinics, and interviewed scores of others in her search for an answer.

Her thesis: "Women are vulnerable to depression because emotional attachments are much more important to them than to men. Women tend to define themselves almost exclusively in terms of their relationships to others. When these bonds break—through death, divorce, or children leaving home—they often suffer depression. Some say they would rather kill themselves than live alone."[1]

Women in today's culture appear to be caught up in a powerful conflict between what their genes are telling them about motherhood and the home, and the current message

125

being sent by society—and especially by women's liberation advocates—that they must get out into the marketplace and compete.

Scarf points out that she found professional women just as subject to depression as those who opted for the more conventional role of homemaker.

SOME CAUSES OF DEPRESSION

The *loss of love* or the *breakup of a relationship* can plunge a woman into the depths of depression. A case in point is that of a woman who had been divorced by her husband. She survived the initial trauma rather well, experiencing only a mild depression. Moving to another city to start life all over again, she formed new friendships and seemed to be doing well. But when a hoped-for love relationship did not evolve as she had hoped, she went into a deep depression. She phoned me one evening before I was aware of her despair. In a choked voice she said, "I'm g-g-going . . . ," then I heard the sound of the receiver being dropped to the floor.

I rushed to her apartment, but as I approached, I saw the flashing red lights of a police car and an ambulance. Two men were coming down the steps bearing a stretcher, and as they passed me, I could see Mona's deathly pale face. I went to the hospital, where physicians were able to pump out her stomach and save her life.

Later I learned from her that before calling me, she had phoned her ex-husband in another city, telling him she had taken an overdose. He alerted the local police, who called for an ambulance.

The call to her former husband was a mixed message, combining a plea for help and muted repressed anger over his having brought her to this. Her phone call to me was simply an announcement that she had taken an overdose but that down deep, she wanted to live. She had never been able to express her anger in the slightest degree. Thus she had gone into suicidal depression.

Luciano Pavarotti, considered by many to be the world's greatest tenor, tells in his autobiography of the depression that overcame him at the very pinnacle of success:

> In the mid-1970's a terrible thing happened to me. I went into a depression. . . . It was unshakable. I am not sure what caused it. I had arrived at the top of my profession.
>
> My family life was wonderful. . . . My three daughters were growing up healthy, bright, and attractive. . . . With all this good fortune, I completely lost my zest for everything. . . . The applause no longer worked like a hypodermic on my system. Everything had lost its point.
>
> I am sure the depression was related to my having succeeded as an opera singer. So many years had gone into the struggle. My whole being had gone into the climb, to the winning of one obstacle and looking immediately toward the next. There were no more obstacles, only the chance of failure. . . . I had no energy and no desire to better myself for any purpose.[2]

Then one night as his plane came in for a landing at Milan, something happened that brought him out of his depression. After a rough landing, the plane broke in two. Panicky passengers were able to escape before the plane burst into flames.

Pavarotti writes: "When I arrived home safe with my family all around me, I realized what an idiot I had been in the past months. I saw how lucky I was; how much love I had, and what a privilege it was to have a gift that made others happy."[3] In the joy over being alive after such a close brush with death, he regained his old familiar state of happiness and contentment.

There are many such instances of people who have gone into deep depression upon reaching some goal. In part it is the result of feeling that they will attain happiness when the objective is reached. But when this happens and there are no bugles blowing—no sudden euphoria—there can be a letdown.

But one of the most common forms of depression results from *repressed anger.*

Those of us who learned in childhood that anger was forbidden, developed the art of repression. This is a process of repudiating the emotion of anger—denying it and refusing to accept it into consciousness.

I learned early in life, at the end of a very big stick, that anger was not permitted. Since legitimate feelings of anger were not allowed, I had no other option but to sulk, which is one of the few choices left to a child who is never permitted to say "I'm angry." In adult life, I learned that when the back of my neck began to tingle, I was angry. I had buried the anger so deeply, I had to await some physical manifestation to tell me I was harboring anger but totally repressing it.

Repressed anger is a denial of reality, a lie to the self. The result can be a migraine headache, ulcers, arthritis, and a host of other symptoms, including numerous types of skin ailments. Anger properly used is of God, given us as a survival instinct, along with all the other valid emotions.

Bury, deny, repress your anger, and you will have either an emotional symptom such as depression, or it will manifest itself in your body in some way.

Depression is not an emotion; it is the feeling one has when emotions are turned off. The emotional structure is overloaded, and one becomes apathetic. Let's look at some other causes of depression.

Another common source of depression is a *sense of guilt* that has been pushed out of consciousness. Guilt is a form of self-hate. When we do not confess it and receive a sense of pardon, it goes underground, and produces—among other things—depression. Thus, depression can often be a helpful warning signal that there is a malfunction—in this case, unconfessed guilt. It can be a guilty act or attitude which we have rationalized. The problem is that the internal judicial system never accepts a rationalization. It knows the truth and rejects our carefully thought out explanations.

A person who fails in some important endeavor feels a sense of loss and accuses himself. *Failure* suggests worthlessness, which is indistinguishable from guilt.

Depression can also be derived from *feelings of rejection.* When we feel unloved, abandoned or that life and people have dealt unjustly with us, we can experience first, anger, which is quickly repressed, then depression. All we are aware of is the fact that we have been hurt in some way and feel depressed.

DEPRESSION, GRIEF, AND DESPAIR

It is well to remember that this depression is an ailment that can be experienced by anyone. In fact, it is not limited to humans. Primates such as chimpanzees are known to suffer from this on occasion. Jane Goodall, who observed them over a period of years in Tanzania, reported a remarkable instance of grief and depression among these interesting animals.

Flo, one of the important senior female chimpanzees in the group, died. Her death was a profound shock to her son, Flint, who had been deeply attached to her. He became very subdued and appeared dejected, overwhelmed by his grief. It was possible to see the utter despair his posture revealed as he walked toward the spot where he had last seen his mother's body before it was taken by the scientists for an autopsy.

His shoulders, his posture, the general slackness of his body, even from the rear at a distance, clearly betrayed his misery. . . . Several days later he was found dead near where his mother had died.

The observers could only assume that he had gone into what proved a fatal depression.

Apparently Flint, a healthy animal, had died of grief.

Rather than being a matter of indulgence, frailty, neurosis, or intransigence, grief becomes a predictable and healthy response to losses of sociobiological consequences, rooted in the body, expressed through it and relevant to its eventual health.[4]

Crossing the highway on foot one day, I saw a strange and interesting sight. A small grass snake had apparently been run over by a car, and its lifeless body lay there, hardening under the hot noontime sun. A live snake of about the same size was curled up alongside it, touching the full length of its body. I don't know what snakes feel, but here beside a lifeless snake was its mate. Do snakes grieve? Are they ever depressed? The living snake obviously felt something akin to what we humans go through when we suffer a loss. Perhaps in some degree, it is common to all living things.

Grief, depression, despair, and hopelessness are often indistinguishable. They are simply different words to describe various aspects of a many-faceted emotion common to humans and even animals.

We read in the New Testament, "Jesus then came with his disciples to a place called Gethsemane. He said to them, 'Sit here while I go over there to pray.' He took with him Peter and the two sons of Zebedee. Anguish and dismay came over him, and he said to them, 'My heart is ready to break with grief ' " (Matthew 25:36-37 NEB).

When adversity or loss bring us to the brink of despair, we can remind ourselves that the Son of God, who was subject to every temptation common to us, also experienced anguish. He had been betrayed by one of his own followers, denied by another, and finally abandoned by them all. "He came unto his own and his own received him not" (John 1:11). When in despair we are prone to ask, "Why should this happen to me?" we can remind ourselves that Jesus endured far more mental, emotional, and physical pain than any of us will ever be called upon to suffer.

IT'S NOT A JUST WORLD

In many ways this seems to be a kind of random universe, where the righteous can suffer while evildoers go about unscathed. But there is the divine promise that ultimately, "They shall never again feel hunger or thirst, the sun shall not beat on them nor any scorching heat, because the Lamb who is at the heart of the throne will be their Shepherd and will guide them to the springs of the water of life; and God will wipe away all tears from their eyes" (Revelation 7:16-17 NEB).

No one ever promised that this would be a just world. There are universal cosmic laws, but they apply to humans in a random way. Life isn't fair. It does not operate according to logic. The Bible tells us, "The race is not to the swift, nor the battle to the strong, nor bread to the wise, nor riches to men of understanding, nor favor to men of skill; but time and chance happen to them all" (Ecclesiastes 9:11).

When an earthquake demolishes a city, it doesn't level the brothels and leave churches standing. A hurricane will demolish the homes of the righteous along with those of evildoers. Jesus pointed out that the rain falls on the just and the unjust, and, of course, the converse is true: A flood may sweep away Christians along with the non-Christians.

When I see a dear, patient saint of God crippled with arthritis or dying of cancer, then learn of a mobster in good health who escapes justice by bribery and the help of high-priced lawyers, I rebel at the injustice of it all.

We see this inequity all around us, and ask, if life is such a hit-or-miss affair, why doesn't God take charge and straighten things out? And what's the advantage of living a Christian life if evildoers are as likely to prosper? Why are children born deformed, mentally retarded, or suffer starvation?

I don't know the answer to sin, suffering, and sorrow, but my own reaction to those very legitimate questions is this:

God *will* take charge. Jesus tells us that Satan is the "prince of this world." But he said he would return one glorious day and reign for a thousand years. "The kingdoms of this world will become the kingdoms of our Lord and of his Christ" (Revelation 11:15).

Another conviction I have is that there is both a present and a future advantage to living the Christian life. To live as followers of Christ gives us the assurance that one day we shall reign with him, in his Messianic kingdom. Meanwhile, living in the light of his teachings and following him to the best of our ability makes for integrity and greater peace of mind. Then, too, through fellowship with Christ we can experience divine guidance. Knowing that we are children of God gives us hope and assurance. Being a loving, compassionate Christian gives us some rich dividends, too. We get love by giving it. Just knowing that we are on the side of the angels brings peace and assurance in an otherwise inscrutable universe.

Finally, there is the divine promise, "God . . . will dwell among them, and they shall be his people, and God himself will be with them. He will wipe every tear from their eyes;

there shall be an end to death, and to mourning and crying and pain; for the old order has passed away!" (Revelation 21:3).

Neurotic Generosity and Depression

I recall a woman whose sense of self-worth was so low that she reacted in a strange and interesting way when her husband asked for a divorce so he could marry a woman with whom he had fallen in love. Helen, the rejected wife, felt utterly devastated, of course, but decided to make the best of it. In doing so, she did a most unusual thing. She learned the name of the woman with whom her husband had fallen love and went to visit her.

Helen relieved the other woman's anxiety by telling her she had come to be of assistance. She then proceeded to tell her competitor how best to get along with her new husband, what to do, what not to do, and assured her she would always be ready to do all that she could to help make the marriage a success.

In dealing with her husband, she was unbelievably understanding and offered him unlimited visiting privileges with the children. She expressed a willingness to be helpful to him in the new relationship; then she went into deep depression.

Her type of depression was the result of repressing her hurt and anger. She had exhibited what some might call Christian love and understanding, but at the price of denying her true feelings. This is not to suggest that she should have expressed her anger inappropriately; it is simply that it is human and normal to *feel* hurt, and thus angry, when one is rejected. To deny these legitimate feelings is to do enormous damage to the emotional structure.

Inquiring about her childhood, I found that her mother had been unable to give love in any form, and her father had been excessively demanding. There was never affirmation or approval in any form from either. Thus, she had grown up without any self-esteem. She had intelligence and a delightful personality, but was utterly devoid of a sense of worth.

I asked her in a counseling session if anyone had ever reflected back to her what they saw in her. She shook her head. I asked, "Would you like for me to mirror back to you what I see in you, including any negative aspects of your personality as well as the positive ones?" With her low self-esteem, she was overcompliant, thus unable to reject any suggestion, and readily agreed.

I then said, "I have gotten to know you quite well in these sessions. There is only one negative trait I see in you. It is your weak self-identity. We normally get a sense of self-worth from our parents. You didn't receive that, and so you are deficient in that area, through no fault of your own."

Then I began to list her many positive traits. She was a warm, sensitive, loving, caring person with genuine ability. I dwelt on various aspects of those personality attributes at considerable length. Without any fulsome praise—for it was unnecessary and would have been inappropriate—I revealed to her what kind of a person she was.

When I had finished, she said, "This is the first time anyone has ever given me an inventory of my personality. I never really knew who I was or what kind of person I was. Your appraisal has been an enormous help."

She wrote later to say that life was taking on a new meaning and that she was handling things with much greater ease. In fact, she sounded positively elated. In responding to her letter, I assured her that, unfortunately, euphoria is an emotional state impossible to maintain, and I would be happy if she could simply live without depression.

PARANOIA AND DEPRESSION

I had occasion over a period of several years to observe the way inferiority and depression work together. A minister with a brilliant mind and tremendous ability accepted a pastorate nearby. He was warmly welcomed by the other ministers, and because of his fine reputation, was asked to speak at several important denominational meetings.

A year or so after his arrival, he said to me in a very melancholy voice that he could see he was not accepted by the other ministers. I asked why he felt that way. He said, "Well, I haven't been asked to speak at any of the conferences lately. For some reason they are rejecting me."

I said, "John, you have been here just about a year, and in that time you have been invited to speak to more denominational gatherings than any other minister. You have been honored and more than accepted."

John said in hurt tones, "But at the last ministers' meeting, I felt totally ignored."

"John, listen: I observed you at that gathering. I stood talking to several men before the meeting opened, and you approached, looking as though you expected rejection, then veered off and walked around us. Why didn't you join the group?"

"No," he said, looking and sounding unutterably depressed, "I could tell by the way the men looked at me that I was not welcome."

I knew this obvious paranoia must have roots in some childhood experience, so I said, "Tell me about your childhood," and he did. He was of German extraction, and as a boy had lived through World War I, when antipathy toward all things German was freely expressed. He was jeered at in school and shunned by his former playmates because of his German ancestry. He spoke of those years with infinite sadness, and I sensed that he had undoubtedly been depressed in some degree all his life. He did not feel intellectually inferior. He knew he had great ability, but the pain of that childhood rejection was feeding the paranoia in his adult personality.

I knew him over a period of about twenty years. During that time, I served on several boards and committees with him, and observed that he always anticipated rejection. The melancholy, depressed tone never left his voice. A man of enormous ability had been marred for life by childhood rejection. He died without ever feeling fully accepted by his peers.

Depression intensifies feelings of inferiority, and one who feels inferior in any degree will often tend to feel depressed. It becomes a vicious circle.

SAINTS CAN BE DEPRESSED

Did the Apostle Paul suffer from occasional feelings of inferiority? One of his letters seems to indicate that he did. This spiritual giant, who wrote a large part of the New Testament and was the chief exponent of Christianity during the early days of the Church, suffered from some severe handicap. We can only guess as to the specifics, but in his second letter to the church at Corinth, he alludes to their criticism of his preaching. They had accused him of being a poor preacher with a weak personality. They also said Paul came across strong in his letters, but he made an ineffective presentation in person. Much of the tenth, eleventh, and twelfth chapters of Second Corinthians are taken up with his defense. He is stung by their criticism and justifies himself. Portions of that letter read as follows:

"I, Paul, appeal to you by the gentleness and magnanimity of Christ—I, so feeble (you say) when I am face to face with you, so brave when I am away. . . . 'His letters', so it is said, 'are weighty and powerful; but when he appears he has no presence, and as a speaker he is beneath contempt' " (II Corinthians 10:1, 10 NEB).

He then proceeds to defend himself, insisting he is not inferior to any of the other apostles or the eloquent speakers with whom they had compared him. Paul apparently was not a great public speaker, at least in the eyes of the Corinthian church. He seems not to have had a strong personality. It is believed by some biblical authorities that Paul had a serious problem with his vision, and perhaps because of this infirmity seemed deficient as a speaker. Was it this physical disability about which he prayed three times, that it might be removed? The answer he received was, "My grace is sufficient for you."

As painful as it must have been for him to be severely criticized for having an ineffectual personality and being a poor preacher, it seems possible that had he been more eloquent, he might not have written so many powerful letters. We might have been denied the wonderful contribution of his writings, had he spent all his time preaching. Even his imprisonment in Rome turned out to be a blessing, as he pointed out. There he had time to write to the churches and encourage them.

Anyone accused of having a personality "beneath contempt" and of being a poor speaker would experience severe feelings of rejection. Paul was far from inferior, but he could not avoid some feelings of inferiority when the Corinthian Christians compared him with the brilliant preacher Apollos and derided him as being deficient in their presence, strong when away. Yes, Paul was stung by their harsh accusation. Who wouldn't be?

When we speak of an inferiority complex, we tend to think of cringing, self-abasing, hand-wringing people who shrink into the background. On the contrary, many eminent people have been tinged with these ubiquitous feelings of low self-worth. And when they are depressed, the sense of inferiority is greater.

Elijah, one of the greatest of the Old Testament prophets, had scored a mighty victory up on Mt. Carmel. Queen Jezebel, the power behind the throne, had her coterie of 850 pagan prophets and priests, who had led the people into idolatry. In an all-day confrontation with the priests, surrounded by a host of dubious observers, Elijah scored a mighty victory when he called down fire from heaven which consumed the offering. The people fell on their faces, crying, "The LORD, he is the God!" (I Kings 18:39).

Elijah, in an all-out effort to rid the country of paganism took the false prophets and priests and had them slain.

When Queen Jezebel heard about it, she sent word that Elijah was going to be executed. Whereupon he took off. He ran as far as he could, then he trotted, then he walked, and finally he holed up in a cave and went into a deep depression. He moaned that he was the last true believer in Israel, and now all was lost. He wanted to die. It was actually a type of suicidal depression. But God dealt with him ever so gently in a "still small voice."

The important thing to recognize is that in his depression, Elijah, despite his magnificent performance a short time before, now felt dejected and hopeless. He didn't have an inferiority complex, but in the depths of his depression, he certainly felt weak, vulnerable, and an utter failure.

COPING WITH DEPRESSION

When depressed people come to our counseling center, our staff always urges them to make no important decisions while they are in a "down period." One's judgment is severely impaired in such a state of mind, and choices made under these conditions are almost certain to lack validity.

Depression is a most uncomfortable state of mind. Actually, it has little to do with the mind. It is the feeling one has when threatening emotions are repressed, and one can feel little or nothing except bleak despair. For whatever comfort it affords us, even the saints and mystics have, in many instances, gone through "the dark night of the soul," when, as one put it, "even godliness seems boring."

I take a very dim view of those who offer simplistic solutions to people suffering from a deep depression. At such a time, advice is futile at best, at worst an insult. Admonitions to pray and read your Bible, to snap out of it, to count your blessings, to take up jogging or meditation, are nearly always worse than a waste of time. Deep depression is a psychological illness that does not yield to easy solutions.

The Apostle Paul, certainly not given to self-pity, writes of his sufferings in Asia, where "we were so utterly, unbearably crushed that we despaired of life itself. Why, we felt that we had received the sentence of death" (II Corinthians 1:9). Whether he is using the editorial "we," is not important. Paul experienced hopelessness, not simply a period of mild depression. Yes, even the spiritual giants can suffer depression and hopelessness when life seems unbearable.

And how, we ask, is all this supposed to help us when we are in the depths of despondency? The only way in which this knowledge can benefit us is in knowing that we are not alone; others have suffered, and we need not blame ourselves for our depression. Nor, need we accept the charge of self-pity when it is hurled at us, nor the fatuous, unsought advice from well-meaning friends who urge us to stop feeling sorry for ourselves.

140

Since depression is experienced subjectively and is invisible to others, the despairing person may be accused of self-pity. Friends or relatives commonly tell such people, "Look on the bright side; don't let yourself feel that way; stop feeling sorry for yourself; count your blessings; think how many millions of people are worse off than you." If one were sick in bed with the flu, there would be get-well cards and sympathetic visitors, but when one suffers far more with depression, few people comprehend the severity of the problem except those who have been there.

In a later chapter, we deal with these and other ways of coping with depression in more detail. For the time being, we will pursue our understanding of the problem.

But more important is the knowledge that people do recover from their depression and their feelings of hopelessness. There is a way out. With patience, forbearance, and faith in the eternal goodness of God, we can survive and find our way out of bleak despair.

The solution, of course, is total honesty with God, self, and at least one other person. This may involve the catharsis of sharing all of one's feeling of hurt and anger. It may also require confession and restitution, or reconciliation. We do these things, not to please God, who after all is getting along quite well; we do it for our own sakes that we may not suffer either depression or some physical symptom. Very often professional counseling is required, in order to avoid the trap of fatuous admonitions or inexpert advice. Fortunately, depression is seldom long-lived. There is an end to it. When we can find the source and deal with the real problem, the depression lifts.

CHAPTER NINE

Developing Self-Esteem

No one commits any act or does any deed, unless the satisfaction outweighs the pain.

Gabriel Montalban

A European woman once wrote me that she had read one of my books and had some questions she wanted answered.

She had been raised in a legalistic church, where the fear of hell was consistently inculcated. In addition, her father had been severely punitive. "Now," she said, "I find myself hating my father and very much afraid of God. I am filled with guilt and self-hate. What shall I do?"

In reply, I urged her to seek a Christian counselor, someone who understood her background and who was competent to advise her. I also suggested a procedure I felt would help her.

THE PRAYER OF AFFIRMATION

I wrote, "At this point in your life, you probably don't even want to forgive your father. I encourage you to utter this prayer of affirmation every day, for at least ninety days: I

141

want to want to forgive my father." I assured her that in time, she would be able to say, "I do forgive him."

She wrote a bit later: "My life has begun to change. I followed your advice, and I have freely forgiven him. Strange that I didn't try this method before, the prayer of affirmation. Also, when I was able to forgive my father in the name of Jesus, I now love him very much. I can't do anything about the past, but I can do something about the present and the future. Another important thing is that I am no longer afraid of God! When I was able to forgive my earthly father and love him, I began to love God instead of fearing him. Now tell me," she wrote, "how can I learn to love myself?"

Our correspondence is still going on as she struggles with this challenging task. It has been somewhat more difficult for her to learn self-forgiveness and love herself, but she reports making remarkable progress. The prayer of affirmation is a highly effective approach.

Even if your problem with inferiority feelings seems overwhelming, you can gain self-esteem by using the same principle. Call it positive thinking or the prayer of affirmation, it amounts to the same thing. Note that many of the psalms are not so much petitions as they are affirmations. Often the writer breaks forth into praise, and then begins to affirm to his emotions what he already knows in his head.

THE DISCIPLINE OF PRIORTIES

There are three main ways of acquiring self-esteem:

1. By having been loved and affirmed as a child, by parents who loved each other and themselves.
2. By osmosis; that is, by observation and imitation. Children tend to acquire self-esteem from warm, loving parents.

3. By one's own achievements. A person with little self-acceptance can develop a positive self-image by reaching worthwhile goals.

One difficulty with the latter is that a person working to achieve a sense of worth may find that it is an endless task. A professional man I once visited had at least thirty certificates on the walls of his office. They attested to the degrees he had received, awards of merit and seminars he had attended. I wondered if he would have felt more okay if he had fifty such certificates instead of thirty.

He *needed* those validations of his worth for he had obviously not been adequately loved and affirmed as a child.

Suppose we back up a bit and take a look at your options. Here are several:

1. You can *retreat* from people, and become a withdrawn personality.
2. You can *advance* in hostility toward people or become manipulative.
3. Or you can *move toward* others in love and friendship, facing life affirmatively, rather than negatively.

Check those three options, and you can see instantly that the last one is the only worthwhile choice.

All right, now that you have decided what your option is to be, let's take a look at your priorities. A hostile young woman from another state had come to our center for help with her troubles and mismanaged life. A large part of her problem was that she was enormously aggressive. Her language was replete with violent obscenities, evidence of the boiling rage within her. Life had not been kind to her, and she felt understandably angry.

From time to time after she left, she wrote ten- to fifteen-page letters brimming with indecision, anger, and a vast melange of disjointed complaints. She would phone from time to time and talk at great length. Her life just didn't seem to fall into place.

Finally she phoned me one evening, and I listened to the plea for help through her verbal barrage. I interrupted at one point and said, "Let's go back a moment. You said that you need to go on and get your degree, find a job and earn a living. Let's focus on that."

She started to zing off into the stratosphere again, but I said, "Hold it! You have stated that your basic need is to finish your education, then get a job. Is that your number one priority?"

"Yes."

"Then," I said, "let's see how you have been sabotaging yourself. You have spent vast amounts of energy fighting institutions and people. You have engaged in vigorous campaigns to help this or that politician to get elected. Now, I want to tell you a great secret: *What you lack is discipline.* Until you become disciplined and focus on one thing at a time, you are going to be a loser.

"Discipline," I said, "means doing what you *ought* to do, when you *ought* to do it, whether you *feel* like it or not."

"Say that again."

I repeated it, and she said it slowly after me. She was strangely quiet, longer than I had ever known her to be. She is a very vocal, aggressive person, and I sensed that I had caught her at a time when she was receptive. I repeated much of what I had said, because she is a much better talker than a listener. She was quite subdued.

"Yes," she said, "I see for the first time what I have to do. I must focus my attention on one thing and not scatter my energies on so many varied interests."

"Right! It's fun to get involved in half a dozen causes and crusades. It suits your aggressive personality, but it doesn't bring in any revenue. It doesn't get you what you want, which is a career that will pay you a decent salary. Focus! Narrow your interests. Give up your crusades to solve the world's problems until you solve your own. When your own life falls into place, you will see more clearly how to help suffering humanity."

"I see," she said quietly.

I said, "I'll pray for you, that you may keep your priorities straight."

"Thanks." She hung up.

Some months later, she wrote to tell me that her life was falling into place and she was becoming more disciplined.

Now, take a look at *your* priorities. What is the primary current need in your life? You may have half a dozen, but you must focus your attention on one at a time. When geese are flying overhead in that fascinating V-formation, the hunter doesn't aim at the flock; he takes a bead on one particular goose. You will have to do the same with your problems and goals. Which one is the most pressing?

If you are troubled about your marriage, the children, finances, conditions at work, relationships with relatives, and a church responsibility, it is obvious that you have to take these problems one at a time. Pick out your primary, fundamental need. Pay attention to that, and work toward a solution. If none is forthcoming immediately, you can always hang the problem on a hook on the left-hand corner of your mind and tackle another issue that seems more likely to be resolved in the immediate future.

FINDING GOD'S WILL

If you are confused, you may need some guidance. You will pray about this, of course, and having prayed, you may feel led to talk with a trusted friend or a professional counselor. The friend may or may not be able to assist you. I would be wary of one who gives too much advice. But you can listen and see if there is any merit to what the friend has to say. Sometimes a sharing group can help one clarify the issues.

Now we come to a *very* important aspect of divine guidance. Some people think that you simply ask, and the answer should come to your mind immediately. It seldom works that way. There is a fundamental principle involved here. It reads: "In all thy ways acknowledge him [God], and he shall direct thy paths" (Proverbs 3:6 KJV). This means that if you earnestly desire divine guidance, you must want God's will in *every area* of your life. You cannot have his will in one aspect of your life if you don't want it in another. You must want his perfect, glorious will in the mental, spiritual, social, domestic, financial, and moral aspects of your life. This is not to say that you will ever live perfectly according to his will. No one has achieved that, except Jesus, but you must *want* it and be willing to pray for it.

Wanting God's will in every area does not mean that change will come all at once. Let's say that there are aspects of your personality you don't like. Perhaps you are timid, depressed, an angry person, or you have some deep seated resentments. You may feel inadequate, insecure, or inferior in some important areas of your life. Pick *one* of those difficulties at a time, and work on it. Suppose you find it difficult to forgive someone. Start there. If your life is cluttered with resentments, some unresolved hostility toward someone, you must *want* to *want* to forgive that person (no matter how justified the anger is). Make that your prayer ten times a day, for ninety days. Say, "Lord, I want to forgive _____." Don't affirm or ask for too many things at once. *Focus* on one thing at a time. Give it your primary attention.

Or let's say you feel inadequate, or have severe inferiority feelings. Having made sure that the channel to God is not choked with resentments, you can pray, "Lord, I want your perfect will in my entire life, and particularly in this painful part. I have inferiority feelings. I want to overcome them. I seek guidance." Make that a consistent, daily prayer. Don't add too many other things. Just focus on that *one thing*. Seek it with all your heart.

In time, as you reflect, pray, and meditate, you will receive an answer, or a gentle nudging in some direction. It may come from a friend, a sermon, something you read or hear. Don't try to predict or predetermine how it should come. Jesus seldom if ever answered any two requests in the same way. He put clay on one man's sightless eyes. Ten lepers were told to go and show themselves to the priests. A lame man was told to take up his bed and walk. Each person is unique, and God deals with each of us in a different fashion.

One Step at a Time

When we observe successful people, it is easy to gain the impression that life has been easy for them. If you were to ask them, many would tell you a different story. Even though some people are especially gifted, the majority of humans have had to struggle to reach their goals.

Phillips Brooks, the greatest preacher of his day, had tried teaching, but he was a total, ignominious failure and returned home in deep depression. He locked himself in his room for several days in utter despair. Later he discovered his true talent and became a positive, radiant, successful personality, but there was a great struggle at first.

Everyone without exception has either suffered the pain of rejection, inferiority feelings, or endured some hardship. Most people, no matter how self-assured they seem, have suffered from self-doubt. Here are some suggestions, gleaned from talking to a great many people who have experienced difficulty in reaching their goals.

Instead of trying to succeed in some outstanding way, take it one step at a time. Choose a goal you can readily attain. In this way you gain additional courage and self-confidence each time you succeed. Having achieved that, try another. Everyone has some talent or ability, or at least the capacity to rack up a minor victory. If you can't win a prize growing the most beautiful dahlias at the county fair, for making the best bird house, or baking the best pie in the bake-off contest, start collecting things—china dolls, match covers, pottery, you name it—the list is endless. You wouldn't believe the things people collect. You can have the best collection of *something* if you work at it. At least it will be a significant one, if nothing else. You will have succeeded, and success breeds success.

Then remember not to boast. Play it cool. Don't hide your light, but don't push it too hard, either. If you can't be the best, you can at least be significant.

That idea may not suit your temperament. Very well, let's try another, something anyone can do. Find some people in your community who are lonely or sick. Visit them regularly. Take a small gift; sit and listen to them. Ask questions. Let them tell you about the things that interest them. Perhaps no one has asked them to do that for years. You become a significant person to them when you listen with genuine interest. And you will get more out of it than they will, for as Jesus said, "It is more blessed to give than to receive." That is, you get more of a bang out of it than the recipient.

Or you can give blood. Everyone has blood, and when you give some away, God creates more for you. During a blood bank campaign in our community, every week at the Family Night Dinner, we asked who had given blood that week. A very timid woman rose one evening and reported that she had given a gallon, and sat down. There was a moment of silence, then she rose again and said, "Oh, not all at one time! Over a period of months." There was laughter and applause. She was a great success in doing something anyone can do—giving blood and lots of it. And it made her feel good.

Something else you can do to gain confidence: Volunteer in your church to do anything the minister or a church officer wants done. It need not be an earthshaking job. Simply offer your services, and you will feel good about having shared in a common Christian enterprise. Get involved. If you believe you have few talents, remember that most human capabilities are learned, not bestowed at birth.

FOCUS ON THE POSITIVES

If you lack self-confidence and have some inferiority feelings, try this practical exercise. Make a list of all your positive attributes—physical, mental, social, spiritual. At first you may think only of your weaknesses. But list only your virtues. If you find it difficult, take the alphabet and try to find one or more positive traits beginning with A. Are you affable, ambitious, amiable, able, agreeable, appreciative, ardent, attentive? Take each letter and rack your mind to find some personality trait that people might find admirable or at least positive.

Add to your list day by day. Keep it with you in your pocket or purse, and jot down your virtues one by one as they occur to you.

I was returning from the East Coast to San Francisco and had a two-hour layover somewhere. I had a terrible cold and felt miserable. I seldom suffer from depression, but as I sat looking bleakly at the mob of people in the airport lobby,

I did feel, if not depressed, at least morbid. And when I feel like that I can find no virtue in myself, only negative attributes. This is the result of lots of hell-fire sermons I heard as a child, plus a punitive parent. So I took a piece of paper from my briefcase and tried to write down some of my virtues. I could think of none, so I took the alphabet, and before long, I had three columns of wonderful, positive qualities. I felt vaguely self-conscious, as though someone were looking over my shoulder and accusing me of vanity, but I stuck to it. I read the list over, feeling much better about myself.

I ran across the list several years later and read it again. "My word," I thought, "this is a pretty good list. Maybe I do have these traits." The list had helped me in a temporary "down" period, and now it gave me a boost years later. So keep your list. Look at it from time to time and glory in your strengths, instead of wallowing in your faults. This is not vanity. It is simply telling your inner self what is true about yourself. You have accused yourself a thousand times of errors, blunders, faults. Now take an honest look at your pluses and thank God for them.

YOU ARE AN IMPORTANT PERSON

I have another suggestion. If your self-esteem is low, think about this: You are not an insignificant person, a mere dot, one of four billion people inhabiting a minor planet in a corner of the universe. Say to yourself, "I am a fragment of the divine. I am a god." (Look it up! It's right there in the Bible in two places: John 10:34 and Psalm 82:61.) "I will be living in God's kingdom through endless eons, when this earth has eroded into dust or has been consumed by fire. When the last star has flamed out and is only a dead cinder, I will be one of the kings and priests unto God, as promised in the Bible (Revelation 1:6 KJV). I am somebody, a body encapsulating an immortal spirit created by almighty God. I am one of his children and worth as much to him as anyone who has ever lived. I have a right to be here!"

Repeat that often! Bask in the divine truths of the Bible. It is the meek who shall inherit the earth, who will reign with Christ when he comes in glory. Say to yourself, "I am worth as much in God's sight as any monarch or potentate who ever lived. Their earthly honors were temporary. The spiritual growth I make in this life is eternal. I am created just a 'little lower than the angels,' and the Bible tells me that one day, I will rule over angels in the Kingdom of my heavenly Father" (Psalm 8).

You know these truths in a general way. Now affirm them by repeating them. To help get this down into your emotional structure so that you can *feel* it as well as *believe* it intellectually, I have some practical suggestions:

STEPS YOU CAN TAKE

Become a knowledgeable person. Anyone can do this. You can become well-informed. The public library is a treasure trove for people who want to learn. You can read voraciously and bone up on current events by reading *Time, Newsweek,* and kindred magazines, and thus be able to hold your own on virtually any topic that crops up in conversation, or, you can pick out one particular subject and learn all about it. Choose a topic that interests you: Ancient Egypt and her pharaohs, archeological discoveries in the Middle East, the history of Rome (almost everyone has forgotten nine-tenths of the history they learned in school). Brush up. You can become an authority on automobiles, nineteenth-century dresses, or early-American cooking—whatever. Choose something that interests you and make youself an authority on that particular subject. Then, my friend, don't bore people to death with your newly acquired fund of information. Just drop the facts in the conversation when it seems appropriate. Your friends are talking about their dogs. Very well, you happen to recall that the Egyptians had some unique breeds of dogs, and now is your chance to share your knowledge.

But you must keep at it. People talk about many subjects. You will want to acquire a vast deal of information on one particular subject and a general fund of information about many things. There is no legitimate excuse for anyone to be ill-informed today. I have known dull, uninteresting college graduates and stimulating, well-informed high school dropouts. We are surrounded by resources—many of them free. If you are in enough pain, you will get to work, for nothing really gets us started on a course of self-improvement except our pain or the dull throb of frustration.

Make others feel significant. Another quality you will want to cultivate is the ability to ask questions. Since the most interesting subject in the world to most people is themselves, you can become an interesting conversationalist by simply asking questions. These must be not probing inquiries, but an effort to draw the other person out. "So you grew up in Wyoming; tell me about it. I don't know much about that part of the country. What's it like?" And when the other person is talking, *listen.* Don't let your eyes glaze over. The query must not be a gimmicky device to start the other person talking while you let your mind wander. If you really aren't all that fascinated, you can fake it until you *learn* to be interested in other people. It is not hypocritical to act appropriately. Get the spotlight off yourself, and you will feel less self-conscious. The best conversationalist asks the best questions.

Making the other person feel significant is not a manipulative device. It is a social interaction method that is a valuable tool in relating positively to people. Practice it. It may take a little while to perfect your technique, so that you feel comfortable with it, but you can in time. You've been hoping someone would focus attention on *you*, and make *you* feel good. Forget it. Make it your goal to help other people feel worthwhile, and you will be a success in human relations.

There are some comments and questions that are verboten. Here is a list of the World's Worst Questions:

Will you promise not to get mad if I ask you something?
Do you have statistics to back up that statement?
You don't honestly expect me to believe that, do you?
Haven't you any sense of humor?
You don't remember me, do you?
Have I kept you waiting?
Now what's the matter?
You asleep?
So what?
When are you going to grow up?

Only by trial and error do we learn some of the important rules of social interaction. If you are afraid of making mistakes, you had better give up all hope of improving your personality and your life situation. Mistakes are not fatal. Consider them simply experiments.

Silent Messages. Then there is the matter of body language. A recent study has demonstrated that the major proportion of our communication is nonverbal. The figures are as follows:

.07 verbal—the words
.37 vocal inflection
.55 body and facial language

Note that 55 percent of our communication is nonverbal. These are the unconscious messages we send by the way we sit, and move, and use our hands, and especially by our facial expressions.

Very often people exude a vague, indefinable something that turns us off. We react to this negatively without knowing why. There is an ancient bit of doggerel written by a Cambridge University student about one of his professors.

> I do not like thee, Doctor Fell,
> The reason why I cannot tell;
> But this I know and know full well,
> I do not like thee, Doctor Fell.

I once knew a man who reacted to almost anything that was said to him with a look of cynicism. I learned later, when we got better acquainted, that he did not have the faintest idea that he acted in that manner. I have known others who have shown suspicious attitudes when any new idea was brought up in committee or board meetings. One insecure man was almost always certain to respond to any new idea with, "Perhaps we should consult an attorney before proceeding with this." A wise friend can point out any unconscious messages you may be sending out.

Unfortunately, as pointed out earlier, most of us would rather be ruined by dishonest praise than saved by honest criticism, but take the risk.

If you have a trusted friend, it can be helpful to ask what kind of an impression you make when you are interacting with somone. Make it clear that you are not asking for compliments, but for an honest reaction to how you come over. If you prefer, have a few sessions with a counselor who will gladly give you his or her professional opinion, reflecting back to you what you are unconsciously conveying.

Sometimes an insecure person will compensate for a real or imaginary deficiency and come on too strong. Nothing is more objectionable than an opinionated or argumentative person. Humility is called for in human relations—not a cringing, self-effacing attitude, but one that is unpretentious.

THE VIRTUE OF GENUINE HUMILITY

Benjamin Franklin now is noted for his wit and aphorisms, but to his contemporaries he was better known for his part in winning the support of France during the Revolutionary War. He was the ambassador to France and made a tremendous hit with his quiet, unassuming approach. He was prone to say in a discussion, "It is quite possible that I am wrong, but it seems to me that this could be a possible solution to the problem." He did not ruffle the feathers of the proud and arrogant with his brilliance, which he kept concealed under his modest demeanor.

The Apostle Paul, one of the greatest minds of his day, and Christ's greatest advocate, could write for all the world to read that he considered himself chief among sinners, and that when he set out to do good, he ended up doing evil. The truly great are not arrogant or conceited.

I have received several hundred letters from readers of my books. I am sure there were readers who disagreed with me on many matters who didn't take the trouble to write. But there was one who did. He wrote an interesting letter, taking issue with something I had written. He ended with this statement: "I feel we must contend for the truth with *relentless fury.*"

I responded, explaining my view of the matter as best I could. He replied that he was not satisfied and wanted to continue the controversy. Finally, I wrote him that anyone who pursues truth with relentless fury is going to have impaired relationships and physical or emotional ailments; that the human organism functions best when we are loving and accepting, but that it malfunctions when we pursue anything with relentless fury. I did not hear from him again.

In your human relationships, avoid controversy. There is a time to stand up for the truth, but people are never convinced of their error by argument. "A man convinced against his will/Is of the same opinion still," said Alexander Pope. Very often people who have a weak self-image, if they get into an argument, feel that they must win or lose face. Arguments divide, love and acceptance unite. There are very few things worth arguing about in the normal course of the day, least of all, the no-win argument as to who was right.

LIMITS TO POSITIVE THINKING

We have been talking in this chapter about building self-esteem through positive thinking. We must face the fact, however, that there are certain limits to positive thinking. Suppose your automobile ran out of gas in the desert. Most of us recognize that we mortals have some limits and are not able to create gasoline out of desert sand.

Jesus could multiply the molecules in a few fish and biscuits and feed five thousand people, but this feat has yet to be duplicated.

Therefore, since there are certain limits to positive thinking, the last chapter deals with the ultimate solution for people who have a serious problem with their self-esteem.

CHAPTER TEN

The Ultimate Cure

Miracles are not always instantaneous. Jesus told us that faith could move mountains, but he did not say it would happen immediately.

Germaine St. Cloud

I will always think of her as the mother who ran away from home. Marion showed up early one Monday morning without warning at our counseling center, asking for help.

Usually, we have a three-to-five-month waiting list, but we were able to fit her in some miscellaneous slots of time. She had left home without telling her husband and children and traveled nearly two thousand miles by bus. Arriving on Sunday, she spent the night sitting in the bus station.

Since the other therapists were all busy, I listened to her story. She had simply gotten fed up with the combination of her lifelong self-hate and her duties as wife and mother. When she couldn't handle the pressure anymore, she decided to go for help. She sensed that if she discussed it with her husband, there might be an argument, so she simply took off. She had read about Primal Integration therapy as practiced at the Burlingame Counseling Center, and thought that this was what she needed.

After her therapy, Marion felt that she could face life

again and went home. She wrote a week or two later:

> I have never been so happy in all my life as when I got home. Everything seemed different when I returned, especially me. And as you know, that's why I went to California, to change me. For the first time in my life, I love myself. Things are so happy here now. My husband and children were amazed at the changes in me. My husband especially likes the way I am now. Everything is new and different between us. We are on a kind of honeymoon. The kids were surprised, too, at the changes in me. I could see it in the way they responded to me. Even their friends asked them what had happened to me.
>
> At church people came up to me and asked what had caused the change in me. Everyone seemed to sense the difference in me. I have never felt so free, so happy, or felt so beautiful in all my life. It was like a dream come true. You wouldn't believe all the things that have happened to me. For instance, my car quit on the expressway, and I, of all people, laughed about it and rejoiced all the way home. That's just one example. . . .
>
> The most important change is between God and me. For the first time in my Christian life, I feel he is actually here, in me, close. I always knew it in my head, but I had never felt his closeness before. My whole Christian attitude changed, and my care for other people has increased. Another unbelievable change has been in my prayer life.
>
> For the first time, I want to do things here at home, for my husband and the children. This was something I never enjoyed before.

We do not relish having people drop in without making arrangements in advance, but an all-knowing God must have had a hand in seeing to it that there was a way to fit Marion into our schedules without too much difficulty. And we were deeply gratified by the transformation in her life.

THE PEARL OF GREAT PRICE

In one of those little gems Jesus was fond of tossing out, he alluded to a merchant in search of fine pearls, who on finding one of great value, sold all that he had to buy it (Matthew 13:45). That's all there is to the story—one single verse—but what a picture! Here is a pearl merchant who saw a pearl of such beauty and perfection that he had to have it. "Save this for me! I'll be back. I must have it!" And he went and sold all his possessions so that he might buy this one glorious gem.

The kingdom of heaven, Jesus said, is like that. It is worth *whatever it costs.* For Marion, that was true of her mental and emotional health. This same principle applies to anything of transcendent importance.

A woman wrote, and later phoned, to tell us about the need she and her husband felt for Primal Integration. Their marriage and her emotional well-being were involved. When she figured up the cost involved of traveling from their home in another state to California, plus the cost of therapy, she said, "I think we can manage it if we sell our car." We told her that we would like to save them as much money as possible and referred them to another counseling center somewhat nearer, where there were several therapists whom we had trained. The director of the counseling center wrote later of the enormous benefit these two desperate people had derived from their therapy. And when I read the report, I thought again of Jesus' brief but powerful reference to the pearl of great price. They had sold their car and entered the Kingdom of wholeness.

LOVE IS EVERYONE'S NEED

There are at least six facets of love that everyone needs in order to develop a healthy self-esteem. Although we have discussed all of them in previous chapters, we will repeat them here. They are:

1. *Affection*—This covers love, warmth, friendship, and sexual response in the marriage relationship.

2. *Approval*—This concerns our need for recognition as persons, not only for our achievements.

3. *Acceptance*—We need this from family, friends, the social group, and fellow workers. I watched a TV program in which a psychologist was interviewing a convicted murderer in his prison cell. The inmate was a nice-looking young man who had received no love or acceptance of any kind at home, and had drifted into the drug culture. There he was befriended by a drug dealer who taught him the trade. He now had a "job," acceptance, and, he thought, a future. In the course of his drug dealings, he shot and killed a man who attacked him. The interviewer asked him what he was searching for when he left home. The young man replied, "Acceptance—someone who cared." As I listened, I sensed that the story would have been far different if his family and friends had given him, if not love, at least acceptance in some form.

4. *Achievement*—Humans are born with the innate drive to accomplish something, to achieve, to solve problems, to learn. Aristotle's term, *entelechy*, describes the growth principle inherent in every living organism. It is the life-growth-achievement principle. When we are able to achieve something worthwhile, we feel gratified with our success. It creates a sense of self-esteem—an awareness of being a worthwhile person.

5. *Acclamation*—Not everyone gets this, but we all hunger for it. Infants being displayed by their mothers for all to admire are at this stage incapable of intellectual thought,

but rest assured of one thing: They are aware of the acclamation. They are being admired, praised. "Such a beautiful baby!" Though they don't understand the words, they grasp the meaning and glow. Whether we call it praise, adulation, applause, or recognition, it is all the same thing—and everyone needs it.

6. *Attention*—Every parent knows full well how much each child needs attention. To be ignored is to feel rejected. The small child needs a vast amount of attention from parents and others to assure him that he is worthwhile. His sense of self-worth grows in proportion as he learns that people pay attention to him. Parents can become grossly irritated and impatient with a child's insatiable need for attention. It is my considered opinion that people who do not have a great deal of patience should never have children. The irritated response of an over-busy parent is perceived by the child as total rejection. This breeds a weak self-esteem.

The child who does not receive an adequate amount of love in most or all of these six ways will become an adult who is either retiring and timid, overly aggressive, or neurotically driven to achieve in order to win approval, acceptance, and recognition. Neurosis is not transmitted genetically, but environmentally. Put simply, most neurosis stems from a lack of love.

I can illustrate from my childhood this voracious need for acclaim. We lived on the edge of a small town. One Saturday morning on my way to the store, I passed through a small wooded area where a four-foot rattlesnake lay in my path. I had seen my father kill rattlers, and I knew precisely what to do. I found a tree limb about the size of my wrist and beat the snake to death. Immediately, I was overcome with a great sense of elation. I had achieved something of significance.

Then came the sobering thought: No one will ever know that I killed this rattlesnake. People will see it lying there in the path, but they won't know that I, Cecil Osborne, performed this mighty deed. There flashed through my mind the childish desire to put up a sign proclaiming the fact that it was I who had met and vanquished this big rattler. Then sanity prevailed, and I went on my way.

When I told my parents about it later, they were busy at other things and had only a moment to say, "That's nice, son; now let me see, where did I put . . . ?" I smile as I recall that incident, but I was not different from the rest of the human race. We all need recognition and affection. A lack of it produces some degree of self-rejection.

RELEASING REPRESSED MEMORIES

Peggy, a minister's wife, had been farmed out to a succession of five different foster homes. In none of them did she feel loved; she was mistreated in all of them. As an adult, she suffered from a number of physical ailments, chief among which was a severe form of arthritis.

In her Primal Integration sessions, Peggy dredged up and relived with terrifying intensity the experience of having been sexually molested in at least four of the five foster homes. Her primals were frightfully intensive, but the results were highly gratifying. She wrote a year later when all physical symptoms had disappeared:

> This has been one of the happiest years of my life. I never realized that getting rid of so much garbage could make such a difference, and I didn't know that I had so much hurt in me. I have listened to the tape recordings of my sessions. I didn't want to believe that had happened, but I know for sure that it did. No one could fake the screams of terror, tears, and total heartbreak that I lived through. I am not that good an actress. I am sorry those things happened to me, but I am able to live with the fact that they did, and even use it,

not only as an aid for myself, but for others. I have shared my experience with people who are crying out for help.

Primal has proven a very effective tool for working with people, much more so than talk therapy. Getting rid of all that fear and anxiety has given me a new zest for life. It feels so good to get up in the morning and feel alive. I feel a new hope in my life, and it's great. Many people have noticed a change in me for the better, and have reported what they see. It's thrilling to know that other people can see what I'm feeling—happiness. . . . My health on the whole has improved almost 100 percent.

Primal Integration was like opening up the drapes and seeing the beautiful sunshine and all the beauty that God has in store for me. I'm glad I learned why I was hurting so much. I have discovered that I am a competent person, and eager to give and gain as much as I possibly can. There was enough pain, hurt, and lack of love in my early years to destroy me. I've always been a person who didn't want to give up, and today I am so thankful that I had the courage to keep on going.

My life has changed so much for the better. I shall always be grateful. . . . If I can use my life's experiences in some way to help others, I shall be glad to do so. I feel free. I feel innocent. I shall not carry any guilt for that of which I am not guilty.

Any emotional trauma, especially if the feelings are buried, tends to upset the normal functioning of the physical organism. Peggy's deprivation of love, coupled with sexual molestation, resulted in serious arthritic symptoms.

The repressed memory of sexual molestation, for another woman, resulted in migraine headaches so severe that the sufferer attempted suicide in a moment of unbearable anguish. After her primal sessions, the migraines vanished.

Physical abuse in childhood has in others resulted in psoriasis and a score of other physical ills. The emotional pain overflows into the body and seeks out the weakest spot. Some suffer depression from physical and emotional abuse as children. A number of people we have dealt with have been so depressed that at times suicide seemed the only way out. Some who suffered abuse or a lack of love as children did not experience physical symptoms but developed personality distortions.

A devout Christian, a counselor by profession, reported with considerable guilt and shame that on several occasions he had struck his wife. She assured him she would divorce him if he didn't get help.

In his primal sessions he relived a very disturbed childhood. His mother, unable to give any love, had provided a distorted picture of marriage. He was projecting onto his wife the buried hate he felt toward his mother.

With great intensity, Henry relived a large number of traumatic episodes with his mother. While he was lying there in a dimly lit room, on a foam rubber mat, he felt himself to be various ages—three, seven, nine—and at times he screamed at his mother with anger that had been repressed for thirty years. It had been leaking out in a distorted form at his wife. Now it was directed at the woman who was responsible for it. With tears of anger and frustration, and finally with violent rage, he told his mother what he had felt during those early years. It was not simply remembered, but relived. Emotions he could not express as a child now came out in violent bursts of hurt and rage.

The marriage is now on firm footing—no more irrational bursts of anger at his wife; all the pent-up anger is gone.

DIVIDENDS FROM UNCOVERING THE PAST

Jack, a serious, somewhat depressed and indecisive professional man, wrote some months after his therapy describing eleven significant dividends he had received from Primal Integration.

"I was suffering from depression and inability to know what to do with my life. I now greatly enjoy life, and I am more in control of it. My physical symptoms—headaches, insomnia, excessive false guilt, anxiety, and sadness—are all significantly improved. I function better at work, my marriage relationship is better, and my self-image is greatly improved. I feel more in touch with God, though I have been a Christian for a long time."

Someone asked me, before beginning therapy, how reliving such scenes from childood could effect a permanent cure. I said, "To put it in simple terms, Primal Integration is a kind of psychic vomiting. If you were nauseated and vomited, that would normally relieve your nausea. Primal Integration is a process of bringing up and discharging accumulated repressed hurts from the past."

"But," the man said, "I remember very little of my childhood. How can I bring up what I have forgotten?"

I said, "Let's listen to a tape recording of a forty-year-old man who came three thousand miles, who experienced events he had completely forgotten. And then we will listen to the tape recording of a woman who came from Hong Kong—one of twenty-four people from there—who relived traumas she never knew she had experienced."

He listened for a few minutes, and said, "Turn it off. I can't listen to that without feeling for those people and for myself. I get the picture. It's the *buried* events that are causing the trouble, and they are dredged up in primal sessions."

"Right," I said, "and it is usually more traumatic to listen to such recordings than it is to experience your own pain, for there is a wonderfully gratifying release when you get in touch with your buried past and discharge the pain surrounding those events."

Larry, a matter-of-fact business man, wrote a year or two following his primal sessions, describing a whole gamut of dividends:

"I have come to know myself, understand myself, and love myself properly because of the primal sessions. It has made me less judgmental. My severe neckaches have been totally cured. The family conflict is gone; I have learned to delegate work in my job, and I have greatly increased my inner peace. I am much more trusting and handle anxiety and anger better. My marriage relationship is improved, and my inferiority feelings are much less. Since ending my therapy, I have led Yokefellow groups, stayed on a diet, and taught a Sunday school class."

THE PRIMAL SCREAM

Annabelle had searched for many years for release from her physical and emotional symptoms. She described a gratifying session with one of our trainees that made everything clear and resolved some lifelong difficulties. Music plays an important part in our type of therapy, and the therapist had chosen the musical composition for this session carefully:

My breathing started becoming more labored, and my body began reacting to fear. I said, "It's the noise. I can't stand it!" and began to scream. The therapist knew I had heard the scream in the music. Suddenly the therapist let out a bloodcurdling scream. Fear shot through me like a bullet. She screamed again and again. Terror shot through me until I thought I couldn't stand the fear. It kept coming, and I started screaming, too. . . . The fear was so strong I feared I was going crazy. Then I became the baby stuck in the birth canal, and I heard a highpitched voice and realized the scream was in my head. I was hearing mother scream during birth. It triggered my pain and fear, but I couldn't scream in the canal.

Each time mother screamed, the canal seemed to tighten, and I was being crushed to death, and my body stiffened. My whole body was reacting to this emergency, which felt like certain death. I felt not only my fear, but my mother's fear that she was dying.

When the pain became too intense, I could feel my infant-self turn off the feelings. My body has always been tense, ready for this emergency. My internal organs were messed up. My digestion has never been right, and there has been a great deal of tension and soreness in the pit of my stomach as long as I can remember.

After I identified the infant's silent screams, I told the therapist that I've listened all my life to hear that scream. I've heard it in certain music and in a dog's barking, and yet all I could do was react in fear to such sounds.

Now a calm has come over me, and . . . there is a rhythm in my body which corresponds to the rhythm in nature. In my primals, I saw nature scenes that tell me that my body is in tune with the rhythm of the universe. I feel life flowing through my body. The repressed pain of birth is over, and my body is now relaxed for the first time. All my life I have felt so geared up that I could find no real rest.

I have always wished I could go away to some island and rest beneath a palm tree on a sandy beach, with the sun warming my body. I wanted the peace that scene portrayed. I couldn't find such peace anywhere. But now I have found the peace which the swaying palm trees symbolized in my fantasy. It's an inner peace now. I feel like a newborn baby, and I'm alive, in tune with nature.

A WHOLE NEW PERSON

As we have seen, failure to receive the necessary affection and affirmation a child needs for proper development can result in a variety of emotional symptoms, such as depression. Gerald wrote of the changes in his personality following primal sessions:

"My friends commented after my Primal Integration session that I was a whole new person. I had been depressed ever since I was six years old, and now the depression is almost completely gone. You told me after one of our sessions that depression is often the result of repressing emotions, and now I have learned to deal with these negative feelings by expressing them appropriately; then the momentary desolation vanishes."

Stella's repressed childhood traumas were the most tragic we have encountered. She is a devout Christian deeply involved in helping promote spiritual growth among a large number of women's groups. She wrote of her Primal Integration experience:

I had been having a problem with severe headaches. For the past twenty-five years, I have had head and body pain that I kept under control with eight to ten aspirins a day. But I finally became immune to all pain medication. I spent a year going from doctor to doctor without success. I was in bed many days, still trying to work with my secretary beside me as I dictated study materials and letters.

After about ten days of therapy at the Burlingame Counseling Center, I began to relive a severe childhood trauma that left me in a critical state for a long time. Sometimes, as I relived that horror, I wondered if I would survive.

Physically, I am in better condition than I have ever been . . . no asthma, no colds, no allergies, headaches much improved. I was never able to walk any distance or exercise because of extreme leg pain . . . and never up hills. While in Califonia, I walked three miles every day and often up to six or eight miles on weekends—many of them were up steep hills.

There was a long-haired cat where I stayed, and I was not in the least allergic to it, as I have always been in the past. I am attending a strenuous aerobic exercise class and find I am able to keep up with the youngest girls. And I am doing 90 sit-ups a day! I lost thirty pounds in California and have gone from a size 12 to a size 6!

Among other things, I am no longer working my way to heaven. I am less critical and judgmental of others. I now understand grace.

BECOMING REAL

A woman wrote:

At the Yokefellow Center, whose therapists you trained, one of them showed me how much buried hostility I had. The idea frightened me, and I refused to believe it. But I felt safe at the center, because I felt so much love from the staff.

Before my Primal Integration therapy, I could not remember any of my past before the age of 9 or 10, and very little between 10 and 13.

Among other things, I relived the repressed trauma of my brother raping me—the brother who later took his own life. I was 13 or 14 when it happened, but I had buried the memory entirely. Then I relived his loaning me out to his friends. I felt dirty, rotten, and ugly. But I couldn't tell anyone, especially my parents. They would have made it seem to have been my fault.

I relived the feeling of fear over hating my brother, for fear of what God would do to me if I hated him, so I not only buried the experience, but the anger as well. Now I can understand why I felt elated upon learning of my brother's death, then feeling guilty over my elation.

There was much more in her letter describing earlier traumas, which had paved the way for her to learn how to block out unpleasant memories. She had to repress the memories in order to survive. She had come to feel inferior, guilty, and worthless. For her the key to becoming a whole person was Primal Integration, which unlocked the door to her tragic past and opened another door to a far better life.

She concluded her letter with this: "Primal Integration

has begun a process within me that has enabled me for the first time to be *real*. I know that this will continue to help me grow and mature into the likeness of Christ."

The Fifty-first Psalm says, "Behold thou desirest truth in the inward being, therefore teach me wisdom in my secret heart" (vs. 6). When the "secret heart," the unconscious mind, gives up its repressed secrets, healing takes place. The psychic pain of self-rejection and inferiority is healed as one relives and thus discharges the anxiety that encapsulates the traumas of childhood.

WHY ARE NOT ALL HEALED?

In most of us there resides some vestigial childhood longing for magic. We would like to be healed instantaneously. A number of successful spiritual healers who have attracted vast crowds to their healing services are unable to explain why only a small proportion of sufferers are healed. Often casual believers or even skeptics are healed, while devout believers are not.

My own tentative explanation, which I have developed in *The Joy of Understanding Your Faith*, is that this phenomenon is attributable, not to capriciousness on God's part, but to the fact that some people are endowed with a native capacity for faith and trust, while others are not.

We read in the New Testament the account of the apostle Paul's visit to Lystra, where "there was a man sitting, who could not use his feet; he was a cripple from birth, who had never walked. He listened to Paul speaking; and Paul, looking intently at him and *seeing that he had faith to be made well*, said in a loud voice, 'Stand upright on your feet.' And he sprang up and walked" (Acts 14:8-10, emphasis added). It is logical to assume that others in that crowd were in need of physical healing.

There are only a few other instances of Paul's healing people, despite the vast need. There are apparently a modest number of people with the innate capacity for deep faith. They are the ones who are usually susceptible to hypnosis, suggestion, and spiritual healing. This does not in any sense deny the fact that it is God who does the healing. Whether a person becomes well physically and emotionally through faith, the ministration of a physician or Primal Integration, it is still God who accomplishes it, using a human as the channel for his power.

When we have a serious physical complaint, we quite wisely make an appointment with a physician. If a kidney transplant is indicated, we may pray for a successful outcome of the operation, but we do not expect God to provide the new kidney.

If there is a serious infection, a physician may prescribe an antibiotic or other medication. It is my conviction that God desires us to become co-creators with him of circumstances. He will not let us become passive, overly dependent persons. When he turned the garden over to Adam and Eve, he made it clear that they were to have dominion over the whole of creation. *They* were to run it and be responsible for the outcome. God's resources were available, and Adam enjoyed a close personal relationship—until the fall. There is no record of such close communion after Adam and Eve were driven from the Garden of Eden. God must have seemed distant after that. As someone has put it: "If God seems far away, who moved?"

For our own growth, it is essential that we learn to be neither dependent nor independent, but become *inter*dependent. God will not do for us what we can do for ourselves.

But I am sure that God yearns over us, longing for our return to fellowship with him. Far more than he wants our service, God desires communion with us. And one fruit of this intimate fellowship is divine guidance—if not an immediate cure for our ills, then either enlightenment as to where to find a solution or patience to endure.

"Prayer changes things" is a popular religious cliche. It would be more apt to say, "Prayer changes people, and people change things," although this is certainly not an all-inclusive statement.

Does this mean that we are not to pray for spiritual, emotional, or physical healing? Not at all. I believe with all my heart in the power of prayer, but we must be open to God's perfect will—rather than insisting that his power be manifested in this or that particular way.

Several million physically disabled people have gone to Lourdes in the hope of being healed. Tens of thousands line up in wheelchairs, litters, and on crutches. The fact that only a minute proportion are healed does not diminish the power of God nor does it demonstrate that he plays favorites.

I can think of no possible explanation other than the fact that we are all different, and that God does not limit his healing to this or that particular method. Relatively few alcoholics are cured of their drinking problem through a sudden, dramatic, religious experience. The vast majority find that they must go to Alcoholics Anonymous. Though AA is the best human resource for this particular ill, even alcoholics admit that only a minuscule proportion of alcoholics are *ever* cured.

We can rest confident that, in the perfect will of God, it was not intended that anyone should suffer. It is in accordance with his will, surely, that *all* should be healed, but he has turned this world over to us, to "have dominion over it." It is our fundamental responsibility to be channels of God's love and healing. He is not going to feed the starving. That is our responsibility. Nor is he going to heal all of the physical and emotional suffering on this tortured planet. If it is done, it is up to us to do it, until that day when "the kingdom of the world has become the kingdom of our Lord and of his Christ, and he shall reign forever and ever" (Revelation 11:15).

Chapter 1

Sources of Weak Self-Esteem

1. Haim Ginott, *Between Parent and Child* (London: Staples Press, 1969).

Chapter 3

How Feelings of Inferiority Reveal Themselves

1. Craig Johnson, *Washington Post* (July 19, 1981).
2. William Sargant, *Battle for the Mind* (New York: Doubleday & Co., 1957)
3. Blaine Goodrich, *Washington Post.*
4. David Riesman, *The Lonely Crowd* (Newhaven, Conn.: Yale University Press, 1950).
5. Alexander Lowen, *The Betrayal of the Body* (London: Collier MacMillan Ltd., 1967).
6. Sargant, *Battle for the Mind.*

Chapter 4

Power, Pride, and Inferiority

1. William Shakespeare, *Measure for Measure*, Act II, Sc. 2.
2. Craig W. Ellison, *Loneliness* (Chappaqua, N. Y.: Christian Herald Books, 1980).
3. *Newsweek* (December 14, 1981).

Chapter 5

Guilt and Self-Esteem

1. Ben N. Ard, Jr., *Counseling and Psychotherapy* (Palo Alto, Calif.: Science & Behavior Books, 1975).
2. Richard P. Walters, *Anger—Yours and Mine—And What to Do About It* (Grand Rapids: Zondervan, 1981).
3. Daniel A. Sugarman and Lucy Freeman, *The Search for Serenity* (New York: Macmillan, 1970).

Chapter 6

Sex and Self-Esteem

1. *Cosmopolitan* (November 1981).
2. Tom Leland, "A Farewell To Prudishness," *Voices* (Spring 1967).
3. Charlie Shedd, *The Stork Is Dead* (Waco, Tex.: Word Books, 1979).
4. Paul L. Warner, M.D., *Feeling Good About Feeling Bad* (Waco, Tex.: Word Books, 1981).

Chapter 7

Self-Esteem and Our Parents

1. Sigmund Freud, in *Dictionary of Psychoanalysis*, ed. Nandor Fodor and Frank Gaynor (Greenwich, Conn.: Fawcett Publications, 1958).

2. Sugarman and Freeman, *Search for Serenity*.
3. Alice Miller, *Prisoners of Childhood* (New York: Basic Books, 1981).
4. Robert Lea, "Why, Deborah?" *Readers Digest* (November 1981).
5. Freud, in *Dictionary of Psychoanalysis*, ed. Fodor and Gaynor.
6. W. V. Caldwell, *LSD Psychotherapy* (New York: Grove Press, 1968).
7. "Dear Abby," *San Francisco Chronicle* (May 2, 1982).
8. Walter Covelle; Timothy Costello; and Fabian L. Ranks, *Abnormal Psychology* (New York: Barnes & Noble, 1960).
9. Karen Horney, *Neurosis and Human Growth* (New York: W. W. Norton & Co., 1950).

Chapter 8

Self-Esteem and Depression

1. Maggie Scarf, *Unfinished Business: Pressure Points in the Lives of Women* (New York: Doubleday & Co., 1981).
2. Luciano Pavarotti, *Pavarotti: My Own Story* (New York: Doubleday & Co., 1981).
3. Ibid.
4. *Psychology Today* (January 1974).